VIRAGO
MODERN CLASSICS

Virago was founded in 1973 in association with Quartet, and became a fully independent company three years later, publishing its first book, *Life as We Have Known It* by Co-operative Working Women in 1977. That book launched the new Virago and The Virago Reprint Library which later included *Maternity* (republished here as *No One But a Woman Knows*). Inspired by, among other things, Sheila Rowbotham's *Hidden from History*, the Virago Reprint Library fed an eager new audience's desire for women's history.

THE CO-OPERATIVE WOMEN'S GUILD

Today, the Co-operative Women's Guild is much smaller than it used to be, with both fewer branches and members; however, its aims and objectives remain the same as when it first started in 1883.

The Guild remains committed to the Co-operative Movement and to helping local communities. It fundraises for chosen local and national charities and campaigns on causes that affect many people, such as recent changes to NHS.

NO ONE BUT A WOMAN KNOWS

Stories of Motherhood
Before the War

Edited by Margaret Llewelyn Davies

virago

VIRAGO

First published as *Maternity: Letters from Working Women* by
Virago Limited in 1978
This edition published by Virago Press in 2012

First published in Great Britain by G. Bell & Sons Limited

Afterword copyright © Gloden Dallas 1978

The moral right of the author has been asserted.

A CIP catalogue record for this book
is available from the British Library.

ISBN 978-1-84408-802-7

Typeset in Goudy by M Rules
Printed and bound in Great Britain by
Clays Ltd, St Ives plc

Papers used by Virago are from well-managed forests
and other responsible sources.

MIX
Paper from
responsible sources
FSC
www.fsc.org   FSC® C104740

Virago Press
An imprint of
Little, Brown Book Group
100 Victoria Embankment
London EC4Y 0DY

An Hachette UK Company
www.hachette.co.uk

www.virago.co.uk

NO ONE BUT A
WOMAN KNOWS

Stories of Motherhood
Before the War

CONTENTS

INTRODUCTION

By Margaret Llewelyn Davies

The whole point of this book lies in the letters which it contains; and it might therefore have seemed advisable to leave the reader untroubled by an introduction to gather that point from the letters themselves. The material is, however, in form and in subject of so unusual a kind that it has been thought necessary to explain something of its origin and its authors, and even to touch upon some of the problems which the letters so vividly show to exist. The letters are written by married women of the working-class, all of whom are or have been officials of the Women's Co-operative Guild. The Guild is a self-governing organisation within the Co-operative Movement, and deals with subjects which affect the Co-operative Movement and the position of married women in the home and the state. It might justly claim to speak with greater authority than any other body for the voteless and voiceless millions of married working-women of England, for it has a membership of nearly 32,000, distributed in 611 branches over the whole country.

The Guild has for several years given special attention to the subject of 'The National Care of Maternity.' Before the Insurance Bill was introduced, the Guild asked for the inclusion of Maternity benefit, and when the Amending Bill was before the House in 1913, an agitation by the Guild secured the benefit as the mother's own property. Later on it placed a scheme for the national care of Maternity before the Local Government Board, which issued a Circular on July 30, 1914, largely embodying the various suggestions of the Guild. In the course of this work it was considered advisable to obtain information from the members themselves of the conditions under which they had brought children into the world. These letters are the result. The barest indication of the information wanted was given, and the only questions used were those on p. 213, as it was thought that it would be more valuable to allow the women to tell their own story in their own way.

We claim for these letters that for the first time are presented in them the real problems of Maternity seen through the women's own account of their lives. If the writers are uneducated in the ordinary sense of school and university, a long schooling in life and suffering has given them a peculiar simplicity and dignity of language in place of the more usual literary style. The letters are left exactly as written by the women, the only alterations made being in the spelling, in the addition of punctuation, and in the omission of a few medical details. All names and places have also been omitted in order to prevent identification.

The women are the wives of men who earn their daily bread by manual labour. The husband's trades cover over one hundred different occupations, and their rates of wages vary from 11s. to £5. The letters show how often the nominal wages are reduced by periods of short time and unemployment, such periods constantly coinciding with childbirth. It should also be remembered that a wife does not usually receive the whole of the weekly wage for her family expenditure.

The earnings and conditions of life of these men are certainly above rather than below the level of their class. It is true on the whole to say that the Co-operative Movement is largely composed of the better-paid manual workers, and there is no doubt that the woman who is secretary of a Guild branch lives in better conditions than the average working woman. If the conditions of their lives are as described in these letters, the suffering and waste of life, the overwork and poverty, must be tenfold and twentyfold where wages are less and employment more precarious. That the women themselves are well aware of this is shown by the occurrence in the letters of such sentences as 'I was more fortunately placed than most women,' or 'I have not had to go through so much pain and suffering as many poor mothers have to go through.'

These letters then give for the first time in their own words the working woman's view of her life in relation to maternity. Now, what is the general impression that the reader gets of the life at such times of these more fortunate working-class mothers? It is on the whole an impression of perpetual overwork, illness, and suffering. The stories and records of 400 lives have been received, taken at random out of the million similar lives lived in our cities. In this book 160 letters have been published, and the unpublished letters describe similar experiences. The evidence of such witnesses cannot be impugned; it is that to bear children under such conditions is to bear an intolerable burden of suffering. The cry of a woman in travail has become a commonplace of literature, and the notion that pain and motherhood are inevitably connected has become so fixed that the world is shocked if a woman does not consider the pain as much a privilege as the motherhood. And this attitude of the world towards the pain of travail has been extended to all the sufferings attending motherhood. These letters show that this is the view of women themselves, for which doctors have been largely responsible. It is hardly too much to say that the ordinary professional attitude might have been summed up in the saying, 'You'll be worse before you're better.' It would be foolish to cry aloud against the inevitable minimum of maternal suffering. And it is to be noted that there is no foolish note of self-pity in these letters. The brave words, combined with a stoic resignation to fate, the invincible optimism shown in such letters as Nos. 32 and 49, are characteristic of the spirit of them all. But if it be folly to kick against Nature's pricks, what is more foolish is the facile fatalism with which we resign ourselves and other people to unnecessary and useless suffering. And a very short consideration of the suffering disclosed in these letters will show that it is both unnecessary and useless.

The roots of the evil lie in the conditions of life which our industrial system forces upon the wage-earners. It is useful to consider the different conditions under which the middle-class and the working-class woman becomes a mother. The middle-class wife from the first moment is within reach of medical advice which can alleviate distressing illness and confinements and often prevent future ill-health or death. During the months of pregnancy she is not called upon to work; she is well fed; she is able to take the necessary rest and exercise. At the time of the birth she will have the constant attendance of doctor and nurse, and she will remain in bed until she is well enough to get up. For a woman of the middle class to be deprived of any one of these things would be considered an outrage. Now, a working-class woman is habitually deprived of them all. She is lucky if her husband hands her over regularly each week 25s. with which to provide a house, food, and clothing, for the whole family. It has to be remembered that the ordinary family wage leaves nothing over for the additional outlay upon maternity. This ought to amount to £5 if the expenses are properly met. Too poor to obtain medical advice during the months of pregnancy, she 'learns by experience and ignorance,' comforting herself with the belief that however ill she be it is only 'natural.' Meanwhile she has to scrape and save to put by money for the inevitable expenses that lie before her. She often goes out to char or sits at her sewing machine, to scrape together a few shillings. She puts by in money-boxes; she lays in little stores of tea, soap, oatmeal and other dry goods. At a time when she ought to be well fed she stints herself in order to save; for in a working-class home if there is saving to be done, it is not the husband and children, but the mother who makes her meal off the scraps which remain over, or 'plays with meat-less bones.' One woman writes: 'I can assure you I have told my husband many times that I had had my dinner before he came in, so as there should be plenty to go round for the children and himself, but he found me out somehow, so that was stopped.' Another woman says: 'Many a time I have had bread and dripping for my dinner before my husband came home, and said I had my dinner, as I would not wait.'

If the mother is not working long hours in a factory, she is working even longer hours in her own home.

Writers on infant mortality and the decline of the birth-rate never tire of justly pointing to the evils which come from the strain of manual labour in factories for expectant mothers. Very little is ever said about the same evils which come from the incessant drudgery of domestic labour. People forget that the unpaid work of the working-woman at the stove, at scrubbing and cleaning, at the washtub, in lifting and carrying heavy weights, is just as severe manual labour as many industrial operations in factories. It is this labour which the mother performs often up to the very day on which the child is born, and she will be at it again perhaps six or eight days afterwards. The Factory Acts make it an offence for an employer knowingly to employ a woman within four weeks after confinement. 'In Switzerland a total absence from employment in factories of women during eight weeks before and after childbirth must be observed, and on their return to work proof must be tendered of an absence since the birth of the child of at least six weeks.' In Germany four weeks' absence is compulsory, and 'must be extended to six weeks unless a medical certificate is furnished approving of employment at the end of four weeks.'

We propose to deal now shortly with the causes of those conditions, then with the results, and finally with the methods of cure and prevention of the resulting evils. The main causes seem to be three:

(1) Inadequate wages.
(2) Lack of knowledge regarding maternity and of skilled advice and treatment.
(3) The personal relation of husband and wife.

We have already dealt to some extent with the first cause. Thirty shillings a week for a manual worker is reckoned to be 'good wages,' and there are, of course, thousands of men earning far less than that. Now, what most people do not realise is that 30s. a week is itself a wage utterly inadequate for rearing a large or even small family. It is inadequate because the whole burden is placed upon the woman who has to bring up a family on 30s., and that burden is excessive. She can only do it at all by incessant labour which inevitably cuts her off from every higher human activity except one. That one which is left to her is maternal affection, and the wonder is that even that endures as it does the strain of poverty, overwork, and illness.

The second cause, the lack of knowledge on the part of the women, receives remarkable testimony in these letters. Again and again the writers come back to this subject. They are convinced of the evils that resulted to themselves and their children from their own ignorance of the functions and duties of motherhood. And there can be no doubt that they are right. Much of the suffering entailed in maternity, much of the damage to the life and health of women and children, would be got rid of if women married with some knowledge of what lay before them, and if they could obtain medical advice and supervision during the time of pregnancy and motherhood. It is not the women's fault that they are ignorant, for the possibilities of knowledge have not been within their reach.

The personal relation of husband and wife is a subject as difficult as it is delicate. Reading these letters one is often struck by the fact that that relation remains so good under the most adverse circumstances. But despite the extraordinary loyalty of the writers, there is clearly a consciousness among them that the position of a woman not only impairs the value of that relationship, but is directly responsible for some of the evils we are considering. In plain language, both in law and in popular morality, the wife is still the inferior in the family to the husband. She is first without economic independence, and the law therefore gives the man, whether he be good or bad, a terrible power over her. Partly for this reason, and partly because all sorts of old half-civilised beliefs still cling to the flimsy skirts of our civilisation, the beginning and end of the working woman's life and duty is still regarded by many as the care of the household, the satisfaction of man's desires, and the bearing of children. We do not say that this is the case in every working-class home, or that there are not hundreds of husbands who take a higher view of married life and practise it. What we do say is that these views are widely held, often unconsciously, and are taken advantage of by hundreds of men who are neither good men nor good husbands and that even where there is no deliberate evil or viciousness, these views are responsible for the overwork and physical suffering among women and for that excessive child-bearing, of which more will be said later.

The effects of the conditions we have described and of the causes which produce them can be conveniently grouped under three heads. They concern, first the woman herself, secondly the children borne by her, thirdly the children that remain unborn of her. So far we have deliberately insisted only upon the evil effects upon the women themselves, and it still remains to insist upon them. The disastrous results of maternal ill-health and overwork upon the children cannot be exaggerated, but in the contemplation of them, people are too apt to forget that the mother herself is an individual with the right to 'equality of opportunity,' which is the right as a human being to be given the opportunity of understanding and enjoying those things which alone make life tolerable to humanity.

It was perhaps inevitable that the mother should have been publicly overlooked, for the isolation of women in married life has, up to now, prevented any common expression of their needs. They have been hidden behind the curtain which falls after marriage, the curtain which women are now themselves raising.

The general effect upon women is the useless suffering inflicted upon them, and one of the chief causes of this is undoubtedly excessive childbearing. This evil is directly due to those semi-civilised notions which were touched upon above, and though, as we shall see when we deal with the decline of the birth-rate, nature is taking her own way of reacting against it, it still exists. We would draw attention to the conditions disclosed in such letters as 1, 20, 36, and 71. In the first case we find a woman married at nineteen having 11 children and 2 miscarriages in 20 years, her husband's wages being 20s. a week. In the second case there are 5 children and one miscarriage in 9 years; in the third 5 children and 5 miscarriages in 12½ years; and in the fourth 9 children and 1 miscarriage in 24 years. These cases have been taken more or less at random, and nothing could be more significant than the bare fact that out of 386 women who have written these letters, 348 have had 1,396 live children, 83 still-births, and 218 miscarriages. These figures speak for themselves: the mere physical strain of pregnancy and childbirth succeeding each other with scarcely an interval for ten or twenty years renders a healthy bodily and intellectual life impossible. And when the additional strain of insufficient means and incessant labour are added, the suffering which becomes the daily concomitant of life is unimaginable to those who are born in the more fortunate classes of society.

If any further evidence is wanted of the direct effect of

such conditions upon the health of women, we would draw attention to the number of miscarriages and stillbirths. It is probable that not all the writers have included miscarriages; but even as it is the number of miscarriages is 15.4 per cent of the live births, while the number of still-births is 5.9 per cent. Taken together, these figures show a prenatal death-rate of 21.3 per 100 live births, as against a national infant death-rate of 10.9. According to some medical writers the frequency of abortions 'is believed to be about 20 or 25 per cent of all pregnancies'; while Dr Amand Routh estimates that the number of deaths during pregnancy probably equals the number of deaths in the first year after birth. The following letters are a pathetic endorsement of the view that fatigue, strain, and domestic conditions are responsible for large numbers of miscarriages, and point to the urgent need of prenatal care.

We have now come by a logical sequence from a consideration of the effect of the conditions of women's lives upon themselves to the further effect upon the life and death of their offspring. We have, in fact, travelled the same road as, but in the opposite direction from, those who in the last ten years have conducted the campaign against Infant Mortality. It was about ten or twelve years ago that many people were suddenly horrified to learn that out of every 1,000 children born in England and Wales, about 150 died before they have lived twelve months. A vigorous campaign against Infant Mortality by means largely of what is called Infant Welfare work followed. Government departments and private persons and organisations have co-operated with such success that the death-rate of infants under one year of age per 1,000 births has fallen from 145 in 1904 to 109 in 1913. But the point which, for our present purpose, is most illuminating is to note the course which that campaign has pursued and is pursuing. It has become more and more clear that if you wish to guard the health of the infant, you must go back from it to the mother; it is the circumstances of the mother – her health, her knowledge, her education, and her habits – before the child is born no less than at the time of and after birth, that again and again determine whether the child is to have health or disease, to live or to die. In fact, from whatever point you regard the question, the words of the writer of letter 62 are true: We shall not get 'a race in the future worthy of England until the nation wakes up to the needs of the mothers of that future race.'

Infant mortality in the first year of life is still appallingly high, and there is good reason for believing – though the fact cannot be absolutely proved – that this high rate is very largely due to the circumstances in which the great mass of working-class women are obliged to bear children. As is well known, it is in the first month after birth that the death-rate is highest, and it is this rate which reformers have been least successful in reducing. Now, if the causes of deaths of infants in the first four weeks of life are examined, an enormous proportion are due to 'immaturity.' 'It needs no argument,' says Dr A. K. Chalmers, 'to show that until we have a clearer conception of the causes which lead to death from immaturity, we cannot but fail to make any considerable impression on the volume of deaths which occur during this period of infant life.' But as a matter of fact there is high authority for debiting the greater number of these deaths from immaturity to the physical health and condition of the mother. 'It is evident,' writes Sir George Newman, 'that if infants die within a few days or hours of birth, or even if dying later show unmistakable signs of being unequal to the calls of bare physical existence, that there must be something more than external conditions or food or management which is working to their hurt. The explanation is clearly to be found in ante-natal conditions.' Dr Noel Paton considers that the 'malnutrition of the mother helps to explain the very high infant mortality among the very poor. The infant starts life at a low level, and readily succumbs to the hardships to which it is too often subjected.' Dr Ashby writes: 'My own experience in the out-patient room entirely confirms the opinion that nutrition of the mother has a very important bearing on the nutrition of the foetus, and that the statement that the percentage of unhealthy births among the poor is small is not justified by facts. We constantly see fully developed infants a day or two old … clearly ill-fitted, as the event proves, to withstand the conditions of external existence ... There is no question of syphilis; they are the children of poor mothers who have lived hard lives of wear and tear during pregnancy, are themselves badly nourished and weakly, and have felt the pinch of poverty, though often perhaps poverty of the secondary sort.'

No better comment upon, or illustration of, these opinions of experts could be found than the facts contained in these letters. You can read in them the little details of existence which made the writers 'mothers who have lived hard lives of wear and tear during pregnancy,' and watching those details you can see how the everyday working of the machine, which we call industry and society, leads to suffering, and wastes and destroys human life as soon as it is born. The results which can already be shown of care in the pre-natal period, bear out the contention that the suffering and loss of life which exists is unnecessary. The Women's Municipal League in Boston, U.S.A., has had 1,512 women in five years (1910–1914) under its care. Amongst these women there have been no miscarriages in the last three and a half years; there were 60 cases of threatened eclampsia in the first year, there were only 2 in the last year; and the total number of infant deaths under one month was 2 per cent, while Boston's rate was 4.3 per cent. The Johns Hopkins Hospital, U.S.A., obtained similar results, and in the Glasgow Maternity hospital more exact methods have reduced the infant mortality and morbidity.

If the problems raised by these letters throw light upon the terrible waste of women's health and infant life, they no less certainly throw light upon another phenomenon of modern society – the decline of the birth-rate.

One of the most remarkable and important signs of change in the habits and aspirations of society, has been the sudden decline in the birth-rate which, noticeable in many countries, began in this country about forty years ago, and has continued steadily down to the present time. In every locality and class the number of children born yearly to married women is declining, but the fall is not the same everywhere; in the industrial population it is greater among the better-class and better-paid workers, and it is distinctly greatest among textile workers where wages are comparatively high and a large proportion of women work in factories. Now, it is absolutely certain that this decline is mainly due to the deliberate limitation of the family. There is, of course, a wide divergence of opinion as to the result of this conscious check upon the growth of population; some regard it as the clearest solution of the inextricable tangle in which the industrial system has enmeshed humanity, others see in it the suicide of a nation and the doom of a race. But people are so anxious to dispute about the good and evil of its effect that they often fail to see that for society itself the important good and evil lie in the conditions which cause the phenomenon. For the State it may be vital to know the result of men and women refusing to give her citizens; but it is still more vital for her to recognize the conditions within her which are leading men and women to this refusal.

These letters give the skeletons of individuals' lives, and individual thoughts and feelings; but in those facts and thoughts and feelings one can see clearly the general mould of life and the sweep of the current of general opinion which is among the working classes, resulting in the refusal to have children. There is a kind of strike against large families, and it is not, among the workers, a selfish strike. The motives of this strike are admirably given in the following words from Letter No. 62, the whole of which is very illuminating on this point: 'All the beautiful in motherhood is very nice if one has plenty to bring up a family on, but what real mother is going to bring a life into the world to be pushed into the drudgery of the world at the earliest possible moment? . . . ' The fact that the decline in the birth-rate is greatest among the better-paid wage-earners is often said to prove that a growing love of ease and luxury is causing a declining birth-rate. The words 'ease and luxury' are grotesque when applied to the lives of manual wage-earners. The fact is that the industrial worker took the first seventy years of last century to learn that the conditions such as described in these letters make a human and humane life impossible alike for the mother and children of large families. This consciousness has spread slowly and surely during the last forty years, and, as is natural, it has spread most amongst the more educated and intelligent workers and those whose wages have given them at least the opportunity of realising that there are other things in life besides poverty and work. The numbers of such men and women will continue to grow who refuse to have children except under two conditions. Those conditions are that society shall pay its debt to the manual worker in such a way that his children can be born into a home where there is something better than bare existence, and that the woman has the means and the leisure to live a life of her own without which she is unfit to give life to her children and to direct it during their most impressionable years.

It is impossible to leave this question without touching upon one point which crops up occasionally in these letters. Opinions may differ as to the good or evil of the general limitation of families, but there can only be agreement upon the evil which results from the use of drugs to procure abortion. There are many facts which go to prove that the habit of taking such drugs has spread to an alarming extent in many places among working women. Several of these letters confirm that conclusion. The practice is ruinous to the health of women, is more often than not useless for procuring the object desired, and probably accounts for the fact that many children are weakly and diseased from birth. But here again the cause of the evil lies in the conditions which produce it. Where maternity is only followed by an addition to the daily life of suffering, want, overwork, and poverty, people will continue to adopt even the most dangerous, uncertain, and disastrous methods of avoiding it.

This introduction has been mainly concerned with pointing out certain evils deeply seated in national life. These evils have their origin in social conditions, and they touch life at so many points that they must, if allowed to work unchecked, modify the whole future of the race and state. There is no sign that society, if left to itself, will secrete some antitoxin to purge its own blood. The industrial and capitalist system tends to become continually more industrial and capitalistic; the gulf between the rich and poor, the fortunate and the unfortunate widens; ideals become higher and broader while the means to satisfy them are narrowed in the possession of a narrow class; only discontent seems to rise while the birth-rate falls. Society cannot cure itself, and the last hope, therefore, is for the State to attempt a cure.

The State has first to realise that if it wants citizens, and healthy citizens, it must make it possible for men and women to have families while living a full life themselves and giving a full life to their children. At the present moment this is not possible from top to bottom of the working class, unless the economic position of the working-class family be improved. The first requisite is, then, the improvement of the economic position of the family.

But it is impossible to treat here the broad question of how this can be attained; it is only possible to deal with the points in which the State can today take immediate steps to improve the economic position of the working-class family as regards maternity, and bring specialised knowledge, adequate rest, nourishment and care, medical supervision and treatment, within reach. And though the story told in these letters, in the statistics of infant mortality, in the figures of a declining birth-rate, be dark, a really bright sign for the future is that the women so vitally concerned have themselves become aware of the evil and are eagerly demanding that the State shall adopt those measures which will most surely mitigate or remove it. The Women's Co-operative Guild have brought out a scheme which would greatly enlarge the scope of State action, precisely in those ways in which it has already proved itself most beneficial. This scheme, which has already to a large extent received the blessing of the Government Department most nearly concerned – the Local Government Board – is given in detail on p. 221. Meanwhile, up and down the country the Guild and other women's organisations are pressing Public Health Committees to adopt the measures recommended. The presence of women on Town and County Councils is another hopeful sign, and it is greatly to be desired that the numbers of working-women councillors will increase. Dr Newsholme says: 'Women could help forward the care of maternity and infants by getting themselves voted on to Local Authorities, and by bringing pertinacious pressure to bear on members of Local Authorities.'

It should be noted that the essence of the Guild scheme is that municipal, not philanthropic, action is wanted. It is not charity, but the united action of the community of citizens which will remove a widespread social evil. The community is performing a duty, not bestowing a charity, in providing itself with the bare necessities for tolerable existence. That is why the end at which the Guild aims is that the mothers of the country shall find themselves as free to use a Municipal Maternity Centre as they are to use a Council School or a Public Library.

The following words of the Chairman of the Bradford Health Committee, spoken at the opening of the Municipal Maternity Home on March 15, 1915, show that the needs expressed in these letters are beginning to be met by the methods desired by the writers: 'We stand on the threshold of an age which is to herald the recognition of the mother and her child, to give public health work that human touch it has hitherto lacked, and to modify those glaring inequalities in social life and conditions which are destructive alike of infancy and the ideals of Christian citizenship.'

Letters from Working Women

1. Twenty years of child-bearing.

I shall be very pleased if this letter will be any help to you. Personally I am quite in sympathy with the new Maternity Scheme. I do feel I cannot express my feelings enough by letter to say what a great help it would have been to me, for no one but a mother knows the struggle and hardships we working women have to go through. I do hope I shall never see the young women of today have to go through what I did. I am a mother of eleven children – six girls and five boys. I was only nineteen years old when my first baby was born. My husband was one of the best and a good father. His earnings was £1 a week; every penny was given to me, and after paying house rent, firing, and light, and clubs, that left me 11s. to keep the house going on; and as my little ones began to come, they wanted providing for and saving up to pay a nurse, and instead of getting nourishment for myself which we need at those times, I was obliged to go without. So I had no strength to stand against it, and instead of being able to rest in bed afterwards, I was glad to get up and get about again before I was able, because I could not afford to pay a woman to look after me. I kept on like that till the sixth little one was expected, and then I had all the other little ones to see after. The oldest one was only ten years old, so you see they all wanted a mother's care. About two months before my confinement the two youngest fell ill with measles, so I was obliged to nurse them, and the strain on my nerves brought on brain-fever. All that the doctor could do for me was to place ice-bags on my head. Oh, the misery I endured! My poor old mother did what she could for me, and she was seventy years old, and I could not afford to pay a woman to see after my home and little ones; but the Lord spared me to get over my trouble, but I was ill for weeks and was obliged to work before I was able. Then in another eighteen months I was expecting another. After that confinement, being so weak, I took a chill, and was laid up for six months, and neighbours came in and done what they could for me. Then there was my home and little ones and husband to look after, as he was obliged to work. It was the worry that kept me from getting better; if I could have had someone to look after me I should not have been so ill. After this I had a miscarriage and another babe in one year and four months. I got on fairly well with the next one, and then the next one, which was the eighth, I had two down with measles, one two years old with his collar-bone out, and a little girl thirteen with her arm broke. That was at the same time as I was expecting my eighth little one, and my dear husband worried out of life, as you see with all this trouble I was only having the £1 a week and everything to get out of it. What a blessing it would have been if this Maternity Scheme was in go then! It would have saved me a lot of illness and worry, for my life was a complete misery. For twenty years I was nursing or expecting babies. No doubt there are others fixed the same way as I have been. This is only a short account of how I suffered; I could fill sheets of paper with what I have gone through at confinements and before, and there are others, no doubt, have felt the pinch as well as myself. If there is anything else you would like to know and I could tell you, I should be glad, for the benefit of my sisters.

Wages 17s. to 25s.; eleven children, two miscarriages.

2. 'Out of bed on the third day.'

I received your paper on Maternity Scheme, and I can assure you it brought back to me many painful hours of what I have passed through in twenty-one years of married life. For one thing, I have had a delicate husband for fifteen years, and I have had nine children, seven born in nine years. I have only one now; some of the others have died from weakness from birth. I only had a small wage, as my husband was then a railway porter. His earnings were 18s. one week and 16s. the next, and I can say truthfully my children have died from my worrying how to make two ends meet and also insufficient food. For many of my children I have not been able to pay a nurse to look after me, and I have got out of bed on the third day to make my own gruel and fainted away. My little girl which is just fourteen years old, from the first month of pregnancy until my nine months were up I attended the hospital and had a hospital nurse in to confine me ... A woman with little wage has to go without a great deal at those times, as we must give our husbands sufficient food or we should have them home and not able to work; therefore we have to go without to make ends meet. Before my confinements and after I have always suffered a great deal with bearing down, and doctors have told me it is weakness, not having enough *good* food to keep my health during such times. My little girl I have was under the doctor for seven months, being a weak child born, and I for one think that if I had a little help from someone I should have had my children by my side today. It has only been through weakness they have passed away. It is with great pleasure I write this letter to you. I could say a deal more on sufferings of women if I saw you.

Wages 16s. to 18s.; nine children, one still-birth,
one miscarriage.

3. Hospitals – a crying need.

A neighbour of mine called in the doctor, who after examining her said she must be got into a Lying-In Hospital at once, as she was in such a critical condition. She needed to be under medical care all the time; the doctor expects when the birth takes place there will be twins. The woman was taken by cab several miles, and after being there two days was sent home, as the birth was not expected till March, and this was about the middle of February; but she was to be taken back by February 27, as she is in such a state that the children will have to be removed before they attain their full size. A few days after she was home, she was so ill that her doctor got a cab and sent her to another hospital, as he said if anything occurred when he was not able to get to her, her life would be lost. She must be where there were doctors in constant attendance.

After putting her through an examination and bullying her for going there, she was informed they had no maternity ward, and sent her home again, and all the time she was in the greatest of pain and vomiting blood; she is now at home, and will have to be taken to the first hospital at the end of the week, if nothing happens before.

Now for her circumstances. Her husband has worked for his present employer for thirteen years, and earns the magnificent sum of 23s. per week. The conveying of her to hospitals and back the two times has cost 25s., and the husband had to lose a day and a half. When the foreman asked the master to allow the man to have his pay for the lost time owing to the expense he had had, he replied: 'He will get 30s. when the job comes off; let him pay it out of that.' This man is a Church warden and a prominent Church worker and Christian! The husband's fellow-workers who earn no more than him, and some of them less, have had what they call a whip round, and have managed to raise 19s. for him.

Our District Nurse goes in each morning and does what she can for her, and one morning she asked how she had got ruptured; and she said she was not sure, but she thought it was when she was at the factory. And it transpired that her eldest boy is very bright, and he managed to win a scholarship, but his mother said she could not manage to get the clothes for him that he ought to have at such a school, and so she got work at the factory to try and clothe him better. She was only there two months when she was taken ill and had to leave. (What mothers put up with for their children!) She has been paying 3d. a week into a Sick Loan, and Dividing Society, in connection with a Church, but she can have no help from it, as her illness is through pregnancy.

4. 'All day washing and ironing.'

In answer to your letter, in my opinion the cause of women suffering from misplacements and various other inward complaints, is having to work during pregnancy, and I am the mother of three children. When the youngest was coming my husband was out of employment, so I had to go out to work myself, standing all day washing and ironing. This caused me much suffering from varicose veins, also caused the child to wedge in some way, which nearly cost both our lives. The doctor said it was the standing and the weight of the child. I have not been able to carry a child the full time since then, and my periods stopped altogether at thirty-four. Then I have a niece of twenty-five, who is at present in hospital undergoing a serious operation through getting up too soon after her confinement. Once we can make men and women understand that a woman requires rest when bearing children, we shall not have so many of our sisters suffering and dying through operations, or, on the other hand, dragging out a miserable existence. My husband's wages was 19s. 10d. He was compelled to lose time in wet or frosty weather, and I was very lucky to get my share, 18s., four weeks in succession.

Wages 19s. 10d.; three children, one miscarriage.

5. A half-starved pregnancy.

My experience during and after my second pregnancy is only one example of what thousands of married working women have to endure. My husband has always been a very delicate man, and was ill most of the time I carried both my children. He had been out of employment eight months out of the nine I carried my first child ... As a last resource was glad to go to work on the railway for the magnificent wage of 17s. a week, and had to walk nearly six miles night and morning or pay 5d. a day for train fare. Our rent was 7s. 6d. a week and clubs to be paid. By the time my second child was born my husband's wages had increased to £1 1s. a week for seventy-two hours. By that time hard work and worry and insufficient food had told on my once robust constitution, with the result that I nearly lost my life through want of nourishment, and did after nine months of suffering lose my child. No one but mothers who have gone through the ordeal of pregnancy half starved, to finally bring a child into the world to live a living death for nine months, can understand what it means ... It was the Women's Co-operative Guild which saved me from despair.

The first confinement I managed to get through very well, having some money left from what I had saved before marriage. But how I managed to get through my second confinement I cannot tell anyone. I had to work at laundry work from morning to night, nurse a sick husband, and take care of my child three and a half years old. In addition I had to provide for my coming confinement, which meant that I had to do without common necessaries to provide doctor's fees, which so undermined my health that when my baby was born I nearly lost my life, the doctor said through want of nourishment. I had suffered intensely with neuralgia, and when I inquired among my neighbours if there was anything I could take to relieve the pain, I was told that whatever I took would do no good; it was quite usual for people to suffer from neuralgia, and I should not get rid of it till my baby was born.

I had to depend on my neighbours for what help they could give during labour and the lying-in period. They did their best, but from the second day I had to have my other child with me, undress him and see to all his wants, and was often left six hours without a bite of food, the fire out and no light, the time January, and snow had lain on the ground two weeks.

When I got up after ten days my life was a perfect burden to me. I lost my milk and ultimately lost my baby. My interest in life seemed lost. I was nervous and hysterical; when I walked along the streets I felt that the houses were falling on me, so I took to staying at home, which of course added to the trouble.

Now, is it possible under such circumstances for women to take care of themselves, during pregnancy, confinement, and after? Can we any longer wonder why so many married working women are in the lunatic asylums today? Can we wonder that so many women take drugs, hoping to get rid of the expected child, when they know so little regarding their own bodies, and have to work so hard to keep or help to keep the children they have already got? If only the

State would do something that would give *all* working mothers the assurance that during pregnancy, where needed, means would be provided whereby they could get an all-important rest before confinement, and that proper attention should be provided during and after so long as necessary. It would make all the difference between a safe and speedy confinement, a better offspring, therefore a better asset of the State, and a broken-down motherhood, and a race of future parents who start in life very often with a constitution enfeebled through the mother having to undergo privation, as well as the mental and physical strain that childbirth entails.

Wages 17s. to £1 1s.; two children.

6. Healthy and strong.

During pregnancy I always looked to my diet, and as my husband never got more than 24s. 6d. per week, I had not much to throw away on luxuries. I had plain food, such as oatmeal and bacon, and meat, plenty of bread and good butter. I may say that during pregnancy and during suckling my appetite was always better, and I ate more and enjoyed my food better than at any other time. I always did my own housework and my own washing, and I never had a doctor all the time I was having children. I have had six, one dead.

During my labour I was never bad more than about

three or four hours. I felt I could get out of bed the first day, and I never had the doctor, only an old midwife.

And though I say it myself, nobody had bonnier or healthier children than I had, with fair skins and red cheeks.

I must say that I am a staunch teetotaller, and have been all my life. I think that drink has a lot to do with some women's sufferings.

I had one child born without a midwife at all, before we had time to fetch her, and I did as well as at any other time.

We lived under the colliery, and our rent was only 3s. 6d. a week. We got our coal at a lower price, about 1s. a week. During part of the time we had a lodger, who paid us 11s., which helped up a bit. But you must know we had to be very careful. But, taking all into consideration, we were very comfortably off. We had not many doctors' bills, as our children were all very healthy, and I don't think I have spent a pound on doctoring for myself since I was a baby, for which I am very thankful.

Wages 18s. to 24s. 6d.; six children.

7. 'She is real ill.'

I have a sister-in-law who has five children, and from the first month of pregnancy she is real ill, the sickness (as she herself puts it) strains her all to pieces, after which she is in a state of collapse. It is painful to be with her, the faint-ness and sickness continue, right up till the eighth month. It is not safe for her to go any distance by herself, as it comes on at any time, and her legs are blue-black until after her baby is born. All her children are living; her con-finements are normal. She is a very plucky woman. Of course, she has to do everything herself; she could not afford to have anyone in to help her, and in that state she has to do all her own washing, cleaning, etc. She has been to the doctor during these bad times, but he does not seem able to relieve her, only tells her to rest her legs all she can, which of course is one of the things with a family around you the mother cannot do. Her husband was only getting 15s. at the time she was having her first three children. Now he is getting £1 per week. He works for the Rural District Council.

Wages 15s.; five children.

8. Men need education.

My own experience in child-bearing was rather abnormal because I had them late in life. Consequently, I suffered more than usual because the bones were set and do not easily adapt themselves to changed conditions. Extreme sickness from first to last, and during last months much pain and much discomfort. My two first were lost from malnutrition because I could not retain my food. In loss of strength the miscarriage cost me most, and because of the falling of the womb – a trouble which was not cured till I had a living child. I was not ignorant, and took every care, so that I can conceive any mother's life being a dreadful thing if she was neglected under such circumstances.

My husband's wages was very unsettled, never exceeded 30s., and was often below the sum. I earned a little all the time by sewing. Did all housework, washing, baking, and made all our clothes. But no amount of State help can help the suffering of mothers until men are taught many things in regard to the right use of the organs of reproduction, and until he realises that the wife's body belongs to herself, and until the marriage relations takes a higher sense of morality and bare justice. And what I imply not only exists in the lower strata of society, but is just as prevalent in the higher. So it's men who need to be educated most. The sacred office of parenthood has not yet dawned on the majority. Very much injury and suffering comes to the mother and child through the father's ignorance and interference. Pain of body and mind, which leaves its mark in many ways on the child. No animal will submit to this: why should the woman? Why, simply because of the Marriage Laws of the woman belonging to the man, to have and to own, etc.

Wages 30s.; three children, two miscarriages.

9. Bad confinements.

I shall only be too glad to assist you in giving my experience. In the first place, I have had eight children; seven is now living. I was twenty-three when I was married. My first pregnancy I suffered with my leg swollen and veins ready to burst. At my confinement the baby was hung with navel cord twice round the neck and once round the shoulder, owing to lifting and reaching, which caused me hours of suffering, and it caused my womb to come down, and I have had to wear something to hold it up until these late years. I am now fifty-eight; my husband has been dead seven years. I was left to fight life's battles alone. As my family increased I had to have my legs bandaged. I never felt a woman during pregnancy; as I got nearer I felt worse. At my confinements the greatest trouble was the flooding after the baby was born, and the afterbirth grown to my side. When that was taken away the body had to be syringed to stop mortification. I have had the doctor's arm in my body, and felt his fingers tearing the afterbirth from my side. While I am writing, I almost fancy I am talking to you. I hope I have not tired you with my letter.

Wages £1 to £2; eight children, two miscarriages.

10. 'I am a ruined woman.'

I have been a martyr to suffering through having children, owing to the fact that I could not retain my food. I was always sick, troubled with nausea and vomiting, which kept me very weak; my constitution was brought that low, that after having three children born living I was unable to go the full length of pregnancy. The last still-born child I had, during pregnancy I was dropsical all the time I was carrying, and I had to have two doctors to chloroform me before the child could be born. It had taken all the water from me; it was impossible for it to be born until they had lanced the child to let the water out of it. I had to be fed every hour day and night. Besides two still-born children, I have had two miscarriages. The last miscarriage I had I lost that much blood it completely drained me. I was three whole months and was unable to sleep; I could not even sleep one half-hour. I had lost my sleep completely; my hair come off and left bald patches about my head. The doctor told me if I had not had the presence of mind to lay me flat on my bed when the miscarriage took place I should have bled to death. Having all this to go through, it brought on falling of the womb, and now that I am able to do for my family and attend to my household duties, I have to wear a body-belt, a kind that is worn after appendicitis. I am a ruined woman through having children. All the times that I was pregnant I could not bear my husband to smoke one pipe of tobacco. I have sent you the main ailments I have had to endure, but there are a hundred and one little items that have crept in between through being brought so weak. I have been subject to other ailments besides, such as influenza, and rheumatic fever, and catarrh of the bowels.

When I was married, my husband was a weaver; at that time his highest wages were £1 per week. We paid 2s. 6d. rent, so that did not leave much for food, fire, and clothing. My first-born was one year all but two days when the second was born. When the last-named was three months old, my husband went on strike for more wages; he was out eleven weeks, and not a penny coming in. At the end of that period, there being both men and women at the same job, the masters were so obstinate they had to go in at the women's price. After the strike there was a turn of bad trade, and he was on short time for seven years; his average wages during that period was 14s. per week. If I had not been a good needlewoman and a capable manager it would have been worse.

Wages £1 to 14s.; three children, two still-births, two miscarriages.

11. 'I was awfully poor.'

My first girl was born before I attained my twentieth year, and I had a stepmother who had had no children of her own, so I was not able to get any knowledge from her; and even if she had known anything I don't suppose she would have dreamt of telling me about these things which were supposed to exist, but must not be talked about. About a month before the baby was born I remember asking my aunt where the baby would come from. She was astounded, and did not make me much wiser. I don't know whether my ignorance had anything to do with the struggle I had to bring the baby into the world, but the doctor said that my youth had, for I was not properly developed. Instruments had to be used, and I heard the doctor say he could not tell whether my life could be saved or not, for he said there is not room here for a bird to pass. All the time I thought that this was the way all babies were born.

At the commencement of all my pregnancies I suffered terribly from toothache, and for this reason I think all married child-bearing women should have their teeth attended to, for days and nights of suffering of this kind must have a bad effect on both the mother and child. I also at times suffered torments from cramp in the legs and vomiting, particularly during the first three months. I hardly think the cramp can be avoided, but if prospective mothers would consult their doctors about the inability to retain food, I fancy that might be remedied. At the commencement of my second pregnancy I was very ill indeed. I could retain no food, not even water, and I was constipated for thirteen days, and I suffered from jaundice. This had its effect on the baby, for he was quite yellow at birth, and the midwife having lodgers to attend to, left him unwashed for an hour after birth. She never troubled to get his lungs inflated, and he was two days without crying. I had no doctor. I was awfully poor, so that I had to wash the baby's clothes in my bedroom at the fortnight's end; but had I had any knowledge like I possess now, I should have insisted at the very least on the woman seeing my child's lungs were properly filled. When we are poor, though, we cannot say what *must* be done; we have to suffer and keep quiet. The boy was always weakly, and could not walk when my third baby was born. He had fits from twelve to fourteen, but except for a rather 'loose' frame, seems otherwise quite healthy now.

My third child, a girl, was born in a two-roomed 'nearly underground' dwelling. We had two beds in the living-room, and the little scullery was very damp. Had it not been for my neighbours, I should have had no attendance after the confinement, and no fire often, for it was during one of the coal strikes. My fourth child, a boy, was born under better housing conditions, but not much better as regards money; and during the carrying of all my children, except the first, I have had insufficient food and too much work. This is just an outline. Did I give it all, it would fill a book, as the saying goes.

In spite of all, I don't really believe that the children (with the exception of the oldest boy) have suffered much, only they might have been so much stronger, bigger, and better if I had been able to have better food and more rest.

Cleanliness has made rapid strides since my confine-ments; for never once can I remember having anything but face, neck, and hands washed until I could do things myself, and it was thought certain death to change the underclothes under a week.

For a whole week we were obliged to lie on clothes stiff and stained, and the stench under the clothes was abominable, and added to this we were commanded to keep the babies under the clothes.

I often wonder how the poor little mites managed to live, and perhaps they never would have done but for our adoration, because this constant admiration of our treasures did give them whiffs of fresh air very often.

My husband's lowest wage was 10s., the highest about £1 only, which was reached by overtime. His mother and my own parents generally provided me with clothing, most of which was cast-offs.

Wages 10s. to £1; four children.

12. 'I dragged about in misery.'

It is lack of knowledge that often brings unnecessary suffering. I know it from experience. In my early motherhood I took for granted that women had to suffer at these times, and it was best to be brave and not make a fuss. Once when things were not brisk in the labour world, I would do my house-cleaning all myself, for naturally at these times you like to feel everything is in order everywhere when the strange woman comes in to take charge. I was in a very weak state through worry and the difficulty of meeting the demands. I had not seen a doctor, for I was thinking of having a midwife I had heard of. I dragged about in misery and in great pain. A friend called in one morning after I had got the children off to school, and I suppose I looked very ill. She said: 'Have you engaged a doctor?' I said: 'No, there is plenty of time; I was only six months, and surely I shall have a change soon.' I could not lay, sit, or stand in ease, and my legs were so bad. However, she went away, saying nothing to me, and brought her doctor. He was amazed at my condition, ordered me to bed, said my confinement was near, and the child was in a critical condition. He sent for a midwife, and they were with me from eleven o'clock till three o'clock. He said the child was dead, and in such an awkward position that it nearly cost my life to bring it. I had a very long illness follow on (it would have been a lovely child full time). The child had been killed through shock, and already showed signs of mortification. I was in a poor state of health, and struggled against my strength, looking after the children's welfare and neglecting myself. In trying to lift the washing-tub it slipped, and that was the shock; and instead of resting and having advice (which I felt I could not afford), I persevered, and that was the result. Now, if there had been such a thing as a Maternity Centre where I could have sent for someone, or could have attended without that feeling of expense, I could have been relieved of all that suffering.

Another experience I had some nine years after the previous. I was pregnant, work had been very scarce, and I was in a very weak state. My husband had been at work three weeks when he happened an accident. He had fallen from a high scaffold. The Clerk of the Works came to tell me they had taken him to the hospital, and I had better go at once and take someone with me. Of course, I thought the worst had happened. (He did not know my condition.) I was between three and four months, and this shock caused a miscarriage. I had a midwife, who, no doubt, was all right when things were straightforward. I got about again, but was very weak and ill. He was in hospital six weeks. I took in needlework. I got very weak yet very stout. I thought it was through sitting so much at the machine. I worked and starved myself to make sick pay, 12s. per week, go as far as possible. I got so weak, and fainted several times after heavy days at the machine. I was taken very ill one night, and my daughter went for the doctor. He said: 'We must have her in bed,' and sent for a neighbour. It was a confinement of a seven-months babe. When he told me it was childbirth, I said it was impossible, for I had miscarried about four months previous. However, it was true. I had been carrying twins – a most peculiar case – during that four months. My system was being drained, and the worry and anxiety had effect on the child. It was weak and did not move much. I had a bad time, but the child lived for nine months, but a very delicate child. Now, if I had been

able to have a qualified midwife when I had the miscarriage, we should have known there was another child, and
if I could have been medically treated, all that suffering
could have been prevented, and I might have had a strong
child.

But apart from all that, I do not know which is the
worst – child-bearing with anxiety and strain of mind and
body to make ends meet, with the thought of another one
to share the already small allowance, or getting through
the confinement fairly well, and getting about household
duties too soon, and bringing on other ailments which
make life and everything a burden. I could forgive a
woman in such a state giving herself and the children a
drug which would end everything. I was an invalid for six
years through getting about too soon and causing womb
displacement.

Wages £2 2s.; eight children, one still-born,
four miscarriages.

13. 'Very fortunate.'

I think I have been very fortunate. I have had two children, both girls; one will be sixteen in April, the other will
be ten in August, so you see there is six years and four
months (and not even a miscarriage) between them. I
have always had the best of health, never had a doctor
until my second baby was born ... When I was married I

was three months short of twenty-one ... Trade was very bad at the time. I worked in the mill up to six weeks from the event; we had a home to make – that is why, as I thought every bit would help. Sometimes we did not make 10s. between us. I had a midwife, and I went on very well; in fact, I asked what I had to stay in bed for. The second day I got up, the fifth day I went out, the seventh baby got on all right, and I went back to work at eight weeks' end. I gave her the breast till she was twelve months old. When weaning her, I put plasters on my breasts, which irritated the skin so much that they brought on inflammation. I suffered awful, as I did not like to tell anybody. It went almost round my body. Then I told mother. When she saw the state I was in she went nearly frantic; she made me go to the doctor, and one box of salve put me right. That is about the worst I suffered with her. I did not even have morning sickness, which I have often heard women speak about during pregnancy, with either of my children. When I was pregnant the second time, I heard that the midwife I had the first time had started drinking, so I was afraid to have her. I had a doctor, and it was well I had, as I did not go on as well as I did the first time. I was in bed a fortnight. I was well looked after, for I have one of the best of husbands and a good mother. I might say I have wanted for nothing. I have two fine girls.

Wages 7s. to 26s.; two children.

14. Inflammation.

When my boy was coming, for three months I could not dress myself properly; I could not get a pair of gloves or boots on, as I was so swollen – I suppose with water. I did not get any advice, as I thought I must just put up with it. After he was born, I could not pass my water for a week – it had to be taken from me. Then I had inflammation of the bladder, and finally inflammation of the kidneys, besides other complications. My doctor, who was an old man, had to leave me in charge of his son for a few days, and once, while talking about my illness, he said it was a blessing I had had the inflammation of the kidneys, as it had disclosed the fact that there was albumen in the water of some standing. I told him how I had been held during pregnancy, and he said I ought to have been to his father at that time, and he would have been able to do me some good, but, like the majority of women, I thought it was one of the ills I *had* to bear.

The next case is of a young married woman with her first baby. She took ill at the eight months, and had a very bad time, falling out of one fit into another, and at last, after her baby was born, she lay two days quite unconscious – in fact, they never expected she would recover. She had two doctors, and they gave her every attention, and then when she was getting better her own particular doctor told her that if she had only consulted him beforehand he could have saved her a lot of pain, which she had to put up with. He said it was some kidney trouble which had been the reason of all she had suffered. In both her case and mine we could have had advice, as far as the expense was concerned, but it was sheer *ignorance, and the idea that we must put up with it till the nine months were over.*

Wages £2; two children.

15. 'Oh, the horrors we suffer!'

From the time I married till just previous to the birth of my third child, my husband earned 28s. per week; then followed two years' shortness of work. When my fourth was born, we had no food or anything to eat, until my husband went to a storekeeper and told him how we were placed, and he trusted us, and said we ought to have asked him before. And we all had dinner off oatmeal gruel made with tinned milk. The past struggle left its mark on the physique of my children. One has since died of heart disease, aged ten years; another of phthisis, sixteen years; my youngest has swollen glands, and not at all robust, though not born in poverty, aged fifteen years ...

I have not been the worst-placed woman by a long way, my husband generally having 30s. per week, but I could not afford help during pregnancy, and I suffer from valvular disease of the heart, which (doctors say) was caused of extreme attacks of haemorrhage and shortness of breath, leaving me a complete wreck at those times. My home was very dirty, the children got ragged, meals worse than usual, and each doctor I consulted said I was not fit to do my work, and I had not to bother. I was told not to worry at all, or I should be worse than I was. No one who has not been placed in a similar position can realise how horrible it is to be so placed. I have resorted to drugs, trying to prevent or bring about a slip. I believe I and others have caused bad health to ourselves and our children. But what has one to do?

I hope this communication will not offend in any way. But after the birth of my first baby I suffered from falling womb, and the torture of that was especially cruel when at closet, in more than I can describe; and quite by accident I learnt that other mothers I met were not suffering the same. My baby was ten months old when I told the doctor, who said I ought to have told him before, and he soon put me right. But doctors who attended me never told me anything concerning my babies or myself. My husband was easeful about attention to himself, and always willing to help, even after working from 6 a.m. in the morning. I often pitied him; he was never impatient. I have seen women similarly placed, and their husbands throw their dinner in the fire. I have been told I ought to do as well as his mother, and I wish I could have done. Oh, the horrors we suffer when men and women are ignorant! Some have severe attacks of haemorrhage caused by sexual intercourse soon after birth ...

Wages 30s.; eight children, two still-born,
three miscarriages.

16. 'A nightmare yet.'

The first feeling of a young mother (to be) (unless she has been very intelligently trained or is very ignorant) is one of fear for herself when she finds out her condition. As time goes on she will probably lose this fear in the feeling she is to have something all her very own, but in some instances the dread grows, and in a sense fills her whole being. This must of necessity weaken her bodily and mentally, and, of course, makes her time of trial harder to bear.

I remember over my first baby, although I felt delighted to think I was to be a mother, I had a very nervous fear that my baby would prove weakly because I had suffered for so many years from chronic bronchitis. I believe this dread had a very bad effect on my nervous system, with the result that when I got within a fortnight of full term my baby was born very weakly, and I had a severe labour lasting two nights and two days. (This was twenty-three years ago.) No effort was made to obtain help for me, although my mother at that time was starting to practise as a midwife, and had all a mother's fears for her daughter in her first labour. At that time it was much more usual to trust to Providence, and if a woman died it only proved her weakness and unfitness for motherhood. My baby only lived seven months. In spite of all this trouble, I was very glad when a year later I found I was to become a mother again. I was still weak, and this baby was born at eight months, very tiny but not weakly. I again had a slow time, lasting two days and one night, but not so severe as the first. I had what is known as 'white-leg' during the lying-in period. This is usually due to a septic condition, and may be induced by uncleanliness or careless handling during the first stage of labour; again, a chill will produce this state, and this was the cause in my case, owing to getting out of bed on the second day rather than call mother upstairs when I needed her. My last baby was born at a time when we were really badly off. My husband was out of work during the greater part of the time, and I was not only obliged to work myself, but often went short of food and warm clothing when I was most in need of it. The effect on my health was, of course, bad, but the baby was a fine healthy boy weighing over 12 pounds. Bad as was the effect on my bodily health, the mental effect was worse. I nearly lost hope and faith in everyone. I felt that even the baby could not make up for the terrible strain I had undergone, and at that time I could fully enter into the feelings of those women who take drugs to prevent birth. I know I ought to have been more strong-minded, but anyway, I got through all right after all, and, strange to say, I got up feeling better and more hopeful than I had felt for years. During this pregnancy I never dared to allow myself to think of the time when the baby would be born; first, because I knew the pain would be so bad, and then because I realised that I would not be able to work when I got near the end and for some time afterwards. I left off a month before and did not start again for four months after the birth. I don't know now *how* I got through, and it is a nightmare to me yet. (I may say here that although we were so poor we stuck to the Store all through, and this was a great help.) I believe if I had felt quite comfortable as to the position of my other children during the time when I would be laid up, my sufferings would not have been so great, or my dread of the labour.

Wages 25s.; three children.

17. Lack of food and bad housing.

I think a great deal of suffering is caused to the mother and child during pregnancy by lack of nourishment and rest, combined with bad housing arrangements. The majority of working women before marriage have been used to stand-ing a great deal at their work, bringing about much suffering which does not tell seriously until after marriage, particularly during pregnancy. A very common complaint is falling of the womb. If women could be taught to sit down more when they were doing little jobs, that they very often stand to do now, I believe it would be a great help to them physically. The majority of working women do not get sufficient nourishment during pregnancy. If there is other children the mother generally takes what is left. I believe this tells very greatly at the time of confinement. I well remember the prostrate condition I have been in on several occasions owing to lack of nourishment and attention at the time. I found I could not get anybody to come into my house and do the work unless I could pay them 10s. per week; in consequence I had to take pot-luck. My last confinement I was nearly twelve months before I was able to do my duties in the home, which meant a great deal of suffering to my children, as they were not kept clean. This caused me a great deal of trouble and anxiety. I believe all this tells on the mother's health and also the baby's which she is nursing. I have known women, who have had the opportunity and good sense, to get all the nourishment and rest during pregnancy, even at the expense of something going short in the home; at time of confinement they have got over it quite easily, and made very little difference to them a few hours afterwards.

I believe the bad housing arrangements have a very depressing effect on mothers during pregnancy. I know of streets of houses where there are large factories built, taking the whole of the daylight away from the kitchen, where the woman spends the best part of her life. On top of this you get the continual grinding of machinery all day.

Knowing that it is mostly women and girls who are working in these factories gives you the feeling that their bodies are going round with the machinery. The mother wonders what she has to live for; if there is another baby coming she hopes it will be dead when it is born. The result is she begins to take drugs. I need hardly tell you the pain and suffering she goes through if the baby survives, or the shock it is to the mother when she is told there is something wrong with the baby. She feels she is to blame if she has done this without her husband knowing, and she is living in dread of him. All this tells on the woman physically and mentally; can you wonder at women turning to drink? If the child lives to grow up, you find it hysterical and with very irritable, nasty ways when in the company of other children. When you see all this it is like a sting at your heart when you know the cause of it all and no remedy.

Wages 28s.; six children.

18. Astonishing health.

Although I have had eight children and one miscarriage, I am afraid my experiences would not help you in the least, as I am supposed to be one of those women who can stand anything. During my pregnancy I have always been able to do my own work.

With the boys labour has only lasted twenty minutes,

girls a little longer. I have never needed a doctor's help, and it has always been over before he came. I have never had an after-pain in my life, so the doctors don't know what I am made of. I always had to get up and do my own work at three weeks' end. I work all day long at house-work until six or seven, and I then take up all voluntary work I can for the sake of the Labour Cause. I am sorry and yet glad that my lot has not been so bad as others. My idea is that everything depends on how a woman lives, and how healthy she was born. No corsets and plenty of fruit, also a boy's healthy sports when she is young. I had the advantage of never having to work before I was married, and never have wanted for money, so when the struggle came I had a strong constitution to battle with it all.

Wages 30s. to 35s., and upwards; eight children,
one miscarriage.

19. 'Kept all to myself.'

I was a very strong woman before my baby was born. I was a weaver. I worked up to five weeks before the baby was born. I had a good appetite all the nine months and did not ail anything. But when baby was born he was a miser-able little thing. Now that I am older I can see things different, and I say that if I had not have worked so hard during the nine months, my baby would have been better.

When a baby is born delicate they are a great care for a good many years.

I may say here that I did not want any more. I never knew what it was to ail anything all my life before, but I could not say that after. I lost 2 stone in weight in a very short time after. Of course, I can see now I was a good bit to blame, because I thought I was only like other women would be, and kept all to myself. I was so strong before he was born, that I was ashamed to own up to it that I felt so weak. It was more weakness than anything else that I suffered from. They used to tell me that I would perhaps be better if I had another, but I said I never would go through it again to feel as bad again. I may say in conclusion, if ever my son takes a wife, I will do all in my power to help her not to suffer as I did.

Wages 20s.; one child.

20. Stead's penny poets.

I was married at twenty-eight in utter ignorance of the things that most vitally affect a wife and mother. My mother, a dear, pious soul, thought ignorance was innocence, and the only thing I remember her saying on the subject of childbirth was, 'God never sends a babe without bread to feed it.' Dame Experience long ago knocked the bottom out of that argument for me. My husband was a man earning 32s. a week – a conscientious, good man, but utterly undomesticated. A year after our marriage the first baby was born, naturally and with little pain or trouble. I had every care, and motherhood stirred the depths of my nature. The rapture of a babe in arms drawing nourishment from me crowned me with glory and sanctity and honour. Alas! the doctor who attended me suffered from eczema of a very bad type in his hands. The disease attacked me, and in twenty-four hours I was covered from head to foot ... finally leaving me partially and sometimes totally crippled in my hands. Fifteen months later a second baby came – a dear little girl, and again I was in a fairly good condition physically and financially, but had incurred heavy doctor's bills and attendance bills, due to my incapacity for work owing to eczema. Both the children were delicate, and dietary expenses ran high. Believing that true thrift is wise expenditure, we spent our all trying to build up for them sound, healthy bodies, and was ill-prepared financially and physically to meet the birth of a third baby sixteen months later. Motherhood ceased to be a crown of glory, and became a fearsome thing to be shunned and feared. The only way to meet our increased expenditure was by dropping an endowment policy, and losing all our little, hard-earned savings. I confess without shame that when well-meaning friends said: 'You cannot afford another baby; take this drug,' I took their strong concoctions to purge me of the little life that might be mine. They failed, as such things generally do, and the third baby came.

Many a time I have sat in daddy's big chair, a baby two and a half years old at my back, one sixteen months and one one month on my knees, and cried for very weariness and hopelessness. I fed them all as long as I could, but I was too harassed, domestic duties too heavy, and the income too limited to furnish me with a rich nourishing milk ... Nine months later I was again pregnant, and the second child fell ill. 'She cannot live,' the doctors said, but I loved ... She is still delicate, but bright and intelligent. I watched by her couch three weeks, snatching her sleeping moments to fulfil the household task. The strain was fearful, and one night I felt I must sleep or die – I didn't much care which; and I lay down by her side, and slept, and slept, and slept, forgetful of temperatures, nourishment or anything else ... A miscarriage followed in consequence of the strain, and doctor's bills grew like mushrooms. The physical pain from the eczema, and working with raw and bleeding hands, threatened me with madness. I dare not tell a soul. I dare not even face it for some time, and then I knew I must fight this battle or go under. Care and rest would have cured me, but I was too proud for charity, and no other help was available. You may say mine is an isolated case. It is not. The sympathy born of suffering brings many mothers to me, just that they may find a listening ear. I find this mental state is common, and the root cause is lack of rest and economic strain – economic strain being the greatest factor for ill of the two.

Working-class women have grown more refined; they desire better homes, better clothes for themselves and their children, and are far more self-respecting and less humble than their predecessors. But the strain to keep up to anything like a decent standard of housing, clothing, diet, and general appearance, is enough to upset the mental balance of a Chancellor of the Exchequer. How much more so a struggling pregnant mother! Preventives are largely used. Race suicide, if you will, is the policy of the mothers of the future. Who shall blame us?

Two years later a fourth baby came. Varicose veins developed. I thought they were a necessary complement to childbirth. He was a giant of a boy and heavy to carry, and I just dragged about the housework, washing and cleaning until the time of his birth; but I looked forward to that nine days in bed longingly; to be still and rest was a luxury of luxuries. Economics became a greater strain than ever now that I had four children to care for. Dimly conscious of the evils of sweating, instead of buying cheap ready-made clothes, I fashioned all their little garments and became a sweated worker myself. The utter monotony of life, the lack of tone and culture, the drudgery and gradual lowering of the standard of living consequent upon the rising cost of living, and increased responsibilities, was converting me into a soulless drudge and nagging scold. I felt the comradeship between myself and husband was breaking up. He could not enter into my domestic, I would not enter into his intellectual pursuits, and again I had to fight or go under. I could give no time to mental culture or reading and I bought Stead's penny editions of literary masters, and used to put them on a shelf in front of me washing-day, fastened back their pages with a clothes-peg, and learned pages of Whittier, Lowell, and Longfellow, as I mechanically rubbed the dirty clothes, and thus wrought my education. This served a useful purpose; my children used to be sent off to sleep by reciting what I had learnt during the day. My mental outlook was widened, and once again I stood a comrade and helpmeet by my husband's side, and my children all have a love for good literature.

Three years later a fifth baby came. I was ill and tired, but my husband fell ill a month prior to his birth, and I was up day and night. Our doctor was, and is, one of the kindest men I have ever met. I said: 'Doctor, I cannot afford you for myself, but will you come if I need?' 'I hope you won't need me, but I'll come.' I dare not let my husband in his precarious condition hear a cry of pain from me, and travail pain cannot always be stifled; and here again the doctor helped me by giving me a sleeping draught to administer him as soon as I felt the pangs of childbirth. Hence he slept in one room while I travailed in the other, and brought forth the loveliest boy that ever gladdened a mother's heart. So here I am a woman of forty-one years, blessed with a lovely family of healthy children, faced with a big deficit, varicose veins, and an occasional loss of the use of my hands. I want nice things, but I must pay that debt I owe. I would like nice clothes (I've had three new dresses in fourteen years), but I must not have them yet. I'd like to develop mentally, but I must stifle that part of my nature until I have made good the ills of the past, and I am doing it slowly and surely, and my heart grows lighter, and will grow lighter still when I know that the burden is lifted from the mothers of our race.

Wages 32s. to 40s.; five children, one miscarriage.

21. How a woman may suffer.

I cannot tell you all my sufferings during the time of motherhood. I thought, like hundreds of women do today, that it was only natural, and you had to bear it. I was left an orphan, and having no mother to tell me anything, I was quite unprepared for marriage and what was expected of me.

My husband being some years my senior, I found he had not a bit of control over his passions, and expected me to do what he had been in the habit of paying women to do.

I had three children and one miscarriage within three years. This left me very weak and suffering from very bad legs. I had to work very hard all the time I was pregnant.

My next child only lived a few hours. After the confinement I was very ill, and under the care of a doctor for some time. I had inflammation in the varicose veins; the doctor told me I should always lay with my legs above my head. He told my husband I must not do any work for some time. I had either to wear a bandage or an elastic stocking to keep my legs so that I might get about at all. I am still suffering from the varicose veins now, although my youngest child is fourteen; at times I am obliged to keep my legs bandaged up. With each child I had they seemed to get worse, and me having them so quickly never allowed my legs to get into their normal condition before I was pregnant again. I do wish there could be some limit to the time when a woman is expected to have a child. I often think women are really worse off than beasts. During the time of pregnancy, the male beast keeps entirely from the female: not so with the woman; she is at the prey of a man just the same as though she was not pregnant. Practically within a few days of the birth, and as soon as the birth is over, she is tortured again. If the woman does not feel well she must not say so, as a man has such a lot of ways of punishing a woman if she does not give in to him ...

Wages 30s. average; seven children, two miscarriages.

22. 'Got on splendidly.'

I have only had one child and one miscarriage, but I can assure you I had such good nursing that I got on splendidly. Of course, I was not allowed to get up before the tenth day, and I do not think that anyone ought to do so, even if they can. I think if everyone at those times had great care and good nursing for a month, there is no reason why they should not get on as well as I did.

One child, one miscarriage.

23. 'One of the fortunate.'

I must be one of the fortunate ones. I have always had fairly good health during pregnancy, and good times at confinements and getting up. I had never had anything to do with children before marriage, and I owe my good health to being well nourished and looked after by my mother when I was a growing girl. I think if the young girls of today are properly cared for, it will make all the difference to the mothers of the future, and save much suffering during pregnancy and after.

Wages 26s. to 30s.; three children, two miscarriages.

24. Utterly overdone.

Sometimes we think that our own life does not seem to be of any importance, and our troubles are what should be, specially before the Maternity Benefit. When I was married, I had to leave my own town to go out into the world, as it were, and when I had to have my first baby, I knew absolutely nothing, not even how they were born. I had many a time thought how cruel (not wilfully, perhaps) my mother was not to tell me all about the subject when I left

In those six years I never knew what it was to have a proper night-sleep. for if I had not a baby on the breast. I was pregnant. & how could you expect the children to be healthy as I always seemed to be half

if I sat- down. I very often fell asleep through the day. I knew any ellte about feeding children; when they cried I gave them the breast; if I had known then what I knows how perhaps my children would have been living. I was ignorant- & had to suffer severely for it; for it nearly cost me my life & also those of my children. I very often ponder over this that I my life. I must. not say any thing about my mother now because she is dead. but I cannot help thinking what - might. have been if she had told me:

home. Although I was twenty-five years of age when married, I had never been where a baby was born. When my baby was born I had been in my labour for thirty-six hours, and did not know what was the matter with me, and when it was born it was as black as a coal and took the doctor a long while to get life into it. It was only a seven-months baby, and I feel quite sure if I had been told anything about pregnancy it would not have happened. I carried a heavy piece of oilcloth, which brought on my labour. Anyway, the boy lived, but it cannot be expected that he can be as robust as if he had been a nine months baby, but he is healthy, but not extra strong.

When he was six years old, I had my fifth baby, and had also a miscarriage, and then I went on strike. My life was not worth living at this rate, as my husband was only a working man, out of work when wet or bad weather, and also in times of depression. I had all my own household work to do, washing, mending, making clothes, baking, cooking, and everything else.

In those six years I never knew what it was to have a proper night's sleep, for if I had not a baby on the breast I was pregnant, and how could you expect children to be healthy, as I always seemed to be tired. If I sat down, I very often fell asleep through the day.

I knew very little about feeding children; when they cried, I gave them the breast. If I had known then what I know now, perhaps my children would have been living. I was ignorant, and had to suffer severely for it, for it nearly cost me my life, and also those of my children. I very often ponder over this part of my life. I must not say anything about my mother now, because she is dead, but I cannot help thinking what might have been if she had told me.

Five children, one miscarriage.

25. Three children in three years.

I was married young. My first three children were born in three years. My husband's wages at that time was 27s. a week. My husband works in a boot and shoe factory. In the winter-time they did not make many full weeks. There were clubs to pay and holidays to provide for. The consequence was my third child was not born strong. She had a cough as soon as she was born. It was a struggle to put enough by to have a nurse in for a fortnight. I have had to get about to do my own housework long enough before I was fit to do it. My last two children have been stronger because I have been able to get better support. My husband was working for Co-operative firms.

When we know what the working women have to go through, you need not wonder at them trying to curtail the family. Though the wages have gone up, it is quite as difficult, for the prices of commodities have gone up too. I do feel that something should be done to help our women, so that they can take better care of themselves during the time of pregnancy. But when they only have the same amount of money coming in, how are they going to do it? For it takes them all their time to keep going on. A mother never thinks of herself. She is always trying to make her family comfortable. A good many of them get about too quick after confinement, and it is making invalids of a good many. I am very sorry I am not in active service for the Guild. I cannot tell you how much I love the work.

Wages 16s. to 27s.; six children, one miscarriage.

26. 'Such is the life of poor women.'

One of the difficulties I experienced during pregnancy was saving the doctor's fee out of the small wage, which was only just enough each week for ordinary expenses. Thanks to the Maternity Benefit, a woman now knows she is provided for at the time.

I have had six children, all living, and what a terrible time it is, to be sure, especially during the last two months – only just enough to live on and another coming. The mental strain in addition to bodily labour must surely affect the child. I think a woman in that state should have all the rest that is possible. I did fairly well for a working man's wife, but the recollection is anything but pleasant. Fancy bending over a washing-tub, doing the family washing perhaps an hour or two before baby is born. I think a woman in that condition should be considered unable to do heavy work for quite six weeks previous to the birth of her child.

Like other wage-paid workers, my husband's wages fluctuated. The unsteadiness of the wages of a labourer is a matter of concern, and working a full week he would scarcely receive a real living wage. During the time of bringing my children up, the highest wage I received in any one week was 30s., and the lowest – well, I had so many that I really do not know how I got through. A week's holiday* meant no wage at the week-end. And if the machinery broke down, or there were strikes or lockouts, it stopped for six clear days, the sum of 10s., and 1s. for each child, would be paid. The same rate would be paid for out of work. My husband was seldom out of work, but, as I have stated, his wage was subject to fluctuation. I think the lowest (not to mention holidays of a week duration, when perhaps I had saved the Dividend to tide the week over) was 4s. 6d.

I shall have to tell you of a case near my home. The woman, I believe, is in her last month. I met her on her way home carrying a baby of two years (her second). She had been out to wash, as she said every copper helped (her husband is a labourer). She said: 'I have to go out as long as I am able to help, to clean or wash; you see, they will not let me work in the factory.' When questioned about

*I.e., an enforced holiday.

the baby she was carrying, her answer was that she took him with her, and he just sits on a chair until she has done. The child in question is rickety. He cannot stand yet. Such is the life of poor women. I have known many such.

27. Worked up to the last.

I will just give you a little of my confinements. I had been married eighteen months when I had my first baby, when I had a trying time, being only an eight-months baby. My water broke five weeks before, and caused what the doctor calls 'dry labour.' He only lived twelve hours. The second came three years and nine months afterwards. I had a straight labour, but I flooded afterwards, and if the doctor had not been there I should have lost my life; it caused me three months' doctoring afterwards. The third one, which came two years and one month after, I had a fairly good labour. Over this one my sufferings were mostly before it came. I had varicose veins in the right leg right away in the abdomen, and the irritation was most distressing; I used to walk the bedroom most nights during the last month. The fourth came two years and three months after the third, and the doctor put me an elastic band on my leg, and of course I did not suffer so much over that one. I could have told at the meeting, where Mrs D. was talking, about babies' eyes, for this one's eyes after a few days began as if they had got cold in them, and the doctor told me then many people took it for cold, but if neglected it was most serious. I am pleased to say I have had no trouble, for he is a fine young fellow now.

Between the fourth and fifth I was four years and eleven months, and then the sixth I went five years and eleven months, and was forty-two when I had him. Of course, I think I am suffering now for some of it, as I have always had to do my own work up to the last, and have had a lot of sickness with my husband and my second boy; till he was eleven years old I scarce ever had the doctor out of the house. I must say that I have had a good husband to help me through, but I do hope we get the £7 10s., and then there will be a many who will not suffer as many poor women have done in the past. At the time I had my children, and weighing all things together, I don't think my husband's wages averaged no more than 28s. a week, lowest 12s. and 15s. I should like to tell you, besides children we had my husband's mother to keep, and allowed her 2s. 6d. a week besides keeping her. He has never been a strong man either, and many a time had him at home six or seven weeks at a time. I feel that when I go to conferences and meetings that I wish I had been a co-operator years ago, for since I have been a Guild worker I feel the years have been wasted, but I am trying to do my best now in my little way. Wishing you every success in the campaign we are fighting.

Wages average 28s.; six children, one miscarriage.

28. Heavy expense of childbirth.

My experiences as a young woman were very difficult, for I was the first child, and had never been brought up with young babies, or afterwards been where they were. My mother dying when I was three years old, I had no one to turn to for advice. I had spent all my youth in the country, and came as a stranger into a strange place, knowing no one but the man I married. My first child was a very delicate child, but I have often thought since that perhaps I had not done all things that were wise, but that would be for want of knowledge. I think a mother is a peculiarity during pregnancy, for I myself never seemed to want anything I had cooked myself, and if I went to any other house I could have eaten the poorest of foods. Then one must not go and buy what we may fancy, as that is an extra expense to the home; and knowing there is an additional expense coming, we have to be very careful. I have not had the Maternity Benefit yet, but that is only a trifle to the large expense that is incurred, when you have paid £1 1s. for your doctor, your nurse 10s. per week, a washerwoman 2s. per day (you cannot get a nurse here under, and if she does the washing she will charge 12s. per week). Then, you never find anyone that makes the money go as far as you do yourself, so that when you get up, instead of having the best of support, and very little to do, you have to begin to get pulled round again, start and do the household work before you are strong enough, with an extra one added. Naturally the child either cannot be nursed by the mother at all, or only partly. The child suffers as well as the mother.

If it could be made possible, I really think mothers should have practically nothing to do with heavy work three months before childbirth and three months after – that is, if life is to be made worth living. But at present we have to clean down thoroughly ready for the event, till I have found myself wondering if death would not be a release. What with worry and feeling bad, I am never surprised at hearing of an expectant mother committing suicide. If she has two or three tiny children, she never has a minute's rest, if she is an energetic housewife.

I think I won't write any more, or you will be thinking I am rather a depressing character, but I shall be glad if anything I have said is any use to others as a benefit in future time.

Wages 20s. to 45s.; five children.

29. 'I am nearly used up.'

Through my married life I have had a good, kind partner, which means so much to the wife, and who always provided me with a doctor and a good nurse for my confinements, which goes without saying that the mother and child have a much better chance than other neglected ones. The first five were born with fifteen months between; then there was a wait of eight years for the sixth, and three years for the seventh. I have always worked hard both before and after childbirth. Give a woman a quiet home and an easy conscience and good plain food, and I see no reason why both mother and child should not do well. Personally, I don't know what I should have done if it had not been for my good old nurse, my dear mother having passed away some years before; but by the grace of God and plenty of common sense, I have brought all my children through so far. I was married in 1884, and knew practically nothing about a child's entry into the world. I do think there should be somewhere where intending brides could get information that would in some way prepare them for what may take place – those who have no mothers, I mean. But so much depends on the woman herself, whether she is going to make the best of things. Personally, I found it was no good worrying, although I found it much harder than most. I never knew what it was to have a day at the seaside for twenty years. I am not grumbling, only now I am nearly used up. If only the Maternity Benefit had been given when I and many others needed it, I cannot help thinking I could have done much better. My husband is a bricklayer, and you may guess it was a bit of a struggle with my little family.

Seven children.

30. 'Mother last.'

When we were first married my husband's wages was £1 a week. I have had seven children; one died at birth, one at one year old, and five are living. Each was about two years and three months old when the other was born. I had one miscarriage, which left me very ill for a long time. I found that the money was so little to do on that I must work as well to pay my way and clothe my children. My husband neither drank or smoked, but when rent, coals, gas, and food is taken out, what was left for other things? I had boarders, and was standing on my legs so much that after the birth of my last child a marble leg set in. I went under an operation, but my leg is still very bad. A mother wants good food before the birth as well as after, but how can it be done out of so little money? If father takes his food it must be as good as can be got; then the children come next and mother last.

Wages 20s.; seven children.

31. Little to tell.

Why is it these things have never been thought of before? Is it ignorance, or is it that people are got used to the idea that we have to expect all sorts of illnesses when a woman gets pregnant, and we have just to put up with it and do the best we can? Personally, I have very little to tell of my own experiences, although I have four children – two boys and two girls, the eldest fifteen years and the youngest six years. Compared with some working mothers, I have gone through those trying periods fairly well. Also my confinements have on the whole been good. My husband's occupation is a carpenter and joiner, and he gets the trade union rate of wages of the district.

Wages, trade union rate; four children.

32. Restriction advocated.

I feel that I must write and explain why I advocate educating women to the idea that they should not bring children into the world without the means to provide for them. I know it is a most delicate subject, and very great care must be used in introducing it, but still, a word spoken sometimes does good. Someone has said that most of the trouble with delicate children were caused by women trying to destroy life in the early days of pregnancy. I do not, of course, recommend that sort of thing. It is absolutely wrong. But it is terrible to see how women suffer, even those that are in better conditions of life. I will quote one or two personal experiences. My grandmother had over twenty children; only eight lived to about fourteen years, only two to a good old age. A cousin (a beautiful girl) had seven children in about seven years; the first five died in birth, the sixth lived, and the seventh died and the mother also. What a wasted life! Another had seven children; dreadful confinements, two or three miscarriages, an operation for trouble in connection with same. Three children died and the mother also quite young. There are cases all round us much worse. You find in the majority of cases that in large families a certain number die and the others have less strength. Of course, there are exceptions. The trouble is that it takes so very long in England for things to be changed, and you are told to mind your own business and let people do as they like; but I am pleased to see that many men and women are getting wiser, to the benefit of the wives and families for whom the poor husband has to provide.

33. 'Almost a wreck.'

I was married at the age of twenty-two (barely twenty-two years), and by the time I had reached my thirty-second birthday was the mother of seven children, and I am sure you will pardon me if I take the credit for bringing up such a family without the loss of even one, seeing that it entailed such a great amount of suffering to myself on account of having to nurse them through all illness, and in addition (after sitting up many nights in succession) being compelled to do all household duties.

During pregnancy I suffered much. When at the end of ten years I was almost a mental and physical wreck, I determined that this state of things should not go on any longer, and if there was no natural means of prevention, then, of course, artificial means must be employed, which were successful, and am happy to say that from that time I have been able to take pretty good care of myself, but often shudder to think what might have been the result if things had been allowed to go on as they were. Two days after childbirth I invariably sat up in bed knitting stockings and doing general repairs for my family. My husband at that time was earning 30s. per week, and out of that amount claimed 6s. 6d. as pocket-money, and when I tell you that through all my difficulties there were no debts contracted on my part, you will be able to form some idea of what women are, in some cases, called upon to endure.

Wages 26s. to 30s.; seven children.

34. Delicate children.

I had my three children in two years and five months, and all the time I carried I had violent sickness, night and day, under a doctor practically the whole time, who, of course, were unable to prevent my suffering. The result was my babies were delicate; the last one suffered with gastritis the whole of its short life – four years and ten months – which ended in peritonitis and abdominal tuberculosis. I have the eldest one still, but he is very delicate and unable to attend school.

Wages 21s. to 27s.; three children.

35. Continual pregnancy for fifteen years.

I can speak from experience. For fifteen years I was in a very poor state of health owing to continual pregnancy. As soon as I was over one trouble, it was all started over again. In one instance, I was unable to go further than the top of the street the whole time owing to bladder trouble, constant flow of water. With one, my leg was so terribly bad I had constantly to sit down in the road when out, and stand with my leg on a chair to do my washing. I have had four children and *ten* miscarriages, three before the first child, each of them between three and four months. No cause but weakness, and, I'm afraid, ignorance and neglect. I was in a very critical state for years; my sufferings were very great from acute weakness. I now see a great deal of this agony ought never to have been, with proper attention. It is good to see some of our women waking up to this fact. It is help and attention during pregnancy that is wanted, and I hope my own dear daughter, if she ever marries, will be one to benefit with others, by our experience. I do hope this letter is something of what you are wishing for, hoping for good results of our Guild work in this matter.

Wages 25s.; four children, ten miscarriages.

36. Many miscarriages.

My experience during wifehood has been that so long as husband and children could have necessities the mother could manage somehow.

It is my silver-wedding day tomorrow, and you will see something of what it has meant to me. I was married young; my husband is five years older. I had my first three children before I was twenty-four, nursing them all. Then I had three miscarriages in the next eight years. I had two more children later, in one and a half years. Since then, eleven years ago, I have had a misplaced womb, and have had two more miscarriages since, one being of twins five months, and one three months.

I believe it was having children too fast that weakened my inside and brought on miscarriages.

When I heard Mrs H. say at our Conference she always had £5 provided for confinement, I felt that she had indeed been a lucky woman. I have never yet been in that position, and it is because a woman has not enough money to pay for things being done for her until she is strong enough to do them for herself, that causes so much suffering.

My husband's wages was 30s. a week when he made a full week, but unfortunately his trade was very uncertain. In ten years we had moved four different times – twice to A, back again to B, and then to C which accounts a great deal for us being short, as we had to pay our own expenses

It is my silver wedding day tomorrow
Monday & you will see by the other
page something of what it has meant
to me.

I was married very young had my
first 3 children before I was 21.
nursing them all. (my husband is
5 years older) then I had 3 miscariages
in the next 8 years. having 2 more
children later in 1½ years
since then. 11 years ago I have
had a misplaced Womb having
to wear an inside article & have
had 2 miscariages since one being
of twins. five months. & one three
months —

I believe it was having children
too fast that weakened my inside

each time, and of course you will understand what it means to a mother when she is left behind. The husband must be found his board-money and pocket-money, even if she goes short of necessaries.

Wages 30s.; five children, five miscarriages.

37. Against large families.

May I say, first of all, that lack of knowledge means, in nearly every case, much unnecessary suffering. I was married at twenty-one, and have had three children – two boys and one girl. Eldest thirty in May, youngest twenty-five. No miscarriages. I might say that I was very ignorant when I was married; my mother did not consider it at all proper to talk about such things. There is too much mock modesty in the world and too little time given to the things that matter. Knowing how ignorant I was on matters of motherhood, my husband bought a book for me called 'Advice to a Wife,' by Dr Henry Pye Chavasse. It is a beautifully written book and would be a gift of untold value to any girl about to marry. There is also a sequel entitled 'Advice to a Mother' – it has saved me pounds of expense – price 2s. 6d., by the same author. Yet, on the other hand, with all this knowledge, I had a very dreadful time with my first child – in fact, I nearly lost my life and reason too, and have never really enjoyed good health since. I was fully six months before I could look after my baby. This was one of my greatest disappointments. I was obliged to put my little one out to nurse, although I had an ample supply of milk. My second and third confinements were very bad, but I was able to get about at the end of the month. It is always a mystery how some poor mothers get about so soon, but of course some women are much stronger than others. Here let me add that through getting about too soon a great deal of suffering is stored up for later years. My old doctor once said to me that if women would only realise that a certain amount of rest was absolutely necessary after confinement, it would add several years to their life. I cannot speak too strongly about the evils of miscarriages. One miscarriage brought about unlawfully ruins a woman's constitution more than half a dozen children. I have suffered from varicose veins since my first child was born, and during pregnancy.

My husband's wages during child-bearing period have been never more than 24s.; being a piece-worker, *has* been as low as 9s. The wages I received when my last child was born (the same week, I mean) were 11s. I was glad to avail myself of a free doctor from the hospital. I may say I had a black doctor, and was never better attended in my life. I do not believe in large families. It does not give either the mother or the children a chance. Here again, I think, much education is needed. Fathers ought to control their bodies for the sake of the mother and child. I could quote several instances where a mother's life has become intolerable through the husband's lack of control. I do trust that the new Maternity Scheme will soon be a fact. I feel that, when put into working order, thousands of poor mothers will be saved unnecessary suffering.

Wages 9s. to 24s.; three children.

38. 'Other children with measles.'

I think the earlier stages of pregnancy are the worst, but a woman needs most attention when she gets up. I have had to nurse my other children with measles when my baby was only four days old. I could never employ a proper nurse. I had six children when my husband was getting £1 a week. I am so glad to see the improvements in the lot of women today, but in some ways it is worse now to bring up a family. I am so glad to see anything being done to help the mother.

Wages £1 and upwards; eight children.

39. Benefit from hearts of oak.

I am afraid I have not much to tell from my experience. I have always been able to look after myself, with the help of a good husband. I have had nine children; eight are living.

When I tell you my husband is a member of the Hearts

of Oak Benefit Society, you will know I have benefited by it.*

Nine children.

40. Neglect by doctors.

I might say that I have had two children. The first one was still-born, but it was owing to the doctor not paying proper attention to me, as, when he came, he said he would not be needed until the morning after. However, I got to be worse, and he was fetched again, but refused to come, so we had to get a midwife, and she said if I had had proper attention the child would have been born then. Consequently, the child was suffocated in the birth. When all was over, my husband went to tell him, and he said he was very glad, as he wanted his rest. Then when I was going to have my second, I ordered another doctor, and when he was wanted, he was drinking, and sent another midwife; so you see I have not had it all straightforward. But when I was carrying them, I can say that I was very well during the time of pregnancy, only for sickness in the morning and after food, until about seven months gone, when I was all right.

Wages 21s. to 23s.; two children.

---

*The Hearts of Oak gives a benefit of 30s. at child-birth.

41. Over-child-bearing.

My feelings during pregnancy were just like those of Mary in Hall Caine ('The Woman Thou Gavest Me'). My mind was full of love and my time of preparation for the coming life within me. I worked very hard during the time of six children, knitting stockings and making clothes for those I already had, so my little one could be well nursed. Three are suffering from consumption, and one from curvature. When I had had six I never murmured, never once said I had enough, and did not want more, but after the birth of my last one I changed, because I could not nurse it and never carried it about. I do not blame my husband for this birth. He had waited patiently for ten months because I was ill, and thinking the time was safe, I submitted as a duty, knowing there is much unfaithfulness on the part of the husband where families are limited.

What is necessary for mothers is State aid for every child she gives birth to. If this is necessary for the aged, it is more so for the mother with the children.

It is quite time this question of maternity was taken up, and we must let the men know we are human beings with ideals, and aspire to something higher than to be mere objects on which they can satisfy themselves. Near my home are two sisters with ten months and eight days between their ages. Two doors from my own are four sisters, all living, and they all came in two years and fifteen days

– the second born eleven months after the first, and thirteen months after twins came, and since then three more have been added to their number. None of them are old enough to work, and you will understand the position of the parents, who are good, deserving, well-meaning people, when the father, being out of work through the war (painter), has had to go labouring.

Wages 30s.; seven children, two miscarriages.

42. 'Constant care and help.'

I take a strong personal interest in the matter, and will state a case that came under my notice, where a poor but respectable mother was practically ill the whole time of pregnancy, gave birth to a healthy baby, herself left very weak, and a month later taken to hospital, as a last resource, from no particular disease whatever. The doctors themselves could not give it a name. I myself should say that all her strength and vitality went to the nourishment of the baby, and she herself was left with scarce enough to live at all. I did all I could. She had another little one, one year and ten months old, at the time. I had him most of the time before her last illness, and entirely during the time she was in hospital (about three months, I think). This happened last year. The baby is now thirteen months old, and a fine, healthy child. The mother is still weak and ailing at times, certainly not fit to attend properly to her home duties and two small children. She had, previously to the two living, two other children, both still-born. In fact, I think both were dead some days previous to birth. This was before I knew her. I am confident, if more help had been forthcoming before and after confinement, she would and could have been saved much suffering.

My own personal experience is small, having had only three and a half years of married life. My one confinement and its results was enough almost for a lifetime. I was not well for many days together the whole time of pregnancy, suffering from sickness, faints, and severe headaches the whole time. A long and severe confinement followed, and a tedious recovery, and I can honestly say that, though it is over two years ago, I can feel the effects of it still, though up till marriage I did not know what illness was. My age was twenty-eight when baby was born. Had I been a poor mother, struggling along on a bare living wage as many are, I do not think I should have been alive now. But constant care and a good, kind husband, and help with the heavy housework when necessary (though I did practically all the work from day to day myself), gave me a far better chance of life and recovery than many, many of our poorer, though equally respectable members have. For they have neither time nor the means, many of them, to take the necessary care of themselves that they should do.

One child.

43. Bad experiences.

When I was married, I left my home and went to a distant town, out of reach of my mother and all my friends, and in due time I became pregnant, and as time rolled on, I began to feel the symptom which I thought was right to feel and bear.

Now, in a strange town, and no particular friends, and, shall I say, mock modest, I was almost afraid to go to a doctor for advice, in case he would think I was a coward, and did not try to bear what I thought was right. At last, I ordered the doctor and midwife, then I awaited the arrival of the baby. The time came. I was in labour thirty-six hours, and after all that suffering had to be delivered by instruments, and was ruptured too badly to have anything done to help me. I am suffering from the ill-effects today. This is thirty-one years ago.

I had two children after that, but all the time I was carrying them I was quite unable to get about. When the last baby was about to arrive, the last month I was not able to go upstairs, unless I got up backwards, and to come down I had to slip from step to step. Going back to the first birth, I was unable to sit down for three months. If I wanted to rest, I had to lie down.

Now, after that experience, my feeling is that if it were possible to get Maternity Centres or schools for expectant mothers, it would be a godsend to many a woman; and also to get some little help in nourishing the body, such as a small quantity of fresh milk. I hope I have enlightened you in some little way; if I have, it is worth the time I have spent in writing.

Wages 26s. to 28s.; three children.

44. 'An indomitable will.'

My health during pregnancy was very good. I took no intoxicants, good, simple food, and through adverse circumstances worked hard in my own home.

I was married in 1887. My husband had just left the Army; he got work as a porter in a bedding warehouse. This firm failed, and he and the book-keeper joined forces and began in the bedding trade in a small way, and we were married. I went every day except Saturday to the shop to cut out and sew. My husband's wages were £1 per week; we did our own housework at night, and I baked and ironed on Saturday morning. When my boy was born, twelve months after marriage, my husband's wages were 25s.; of course, I could earn nothing. In another twelve months my second baby (a girl) was born. We removed to ——, where rents were cheap, and I was a stranger. I took in plain sewing and washing, and cut up my clothes for my babies. I had a good stock of clothes, I may say.

About this time we were involved in a lawsuit which

was quite unnecessary, and our income was reduced to 19s. 6d. per week. I still took what work I could get, minded a child whose mother worked in the mill, etc. I had no assistance from my own family, as I was too proud to let them know. This lasted three years, when we had a change for the better. The cost of this lawsuit I mentioned was, to us, £55 12s. 4d. I then had another daughter, and three years later another girl. I could then obtain one dozen pounds of sugar for 1s 9d., now it is 4s., and this applies to many things. When my last baby was born my housekeeping money was £2 10s.

The first six years of my married life was one perpetual struggle, often wanting necessaries, but God's hand has been over it all, and I thank Him today for the faith and perseverance with which I was enabled to go through this struggle.

Our circumstances are improved, and my three daughters are all teachers – one certificated, and one college-trained, the youngest a student teacher, entering College in September next. Two of my girls are accomplished musicians, and can do anything menial or otherwise in a home. I think if the mothers of today were not so idle it would be better for them; also, if they would make their own food, and not buy ready-made food, we should have a better class of children and healthy mothers. I am fifty-three next month, do my own washing, baking, and cleaning with a little help from my girls. My house has nine rooms and three cellars. I still make time to do my secretarial duties, and take a great interest therein. I was an extremely delicate girl, and suffered from heart disease as a child, but my doctor says I have a most indomitable will. Lest you should think I am of a boasting nature, I beg to submit that God has been very merciful and kind to me.

Wages £1 to over £2 10s.; four children.

45. 'Mock modesty.'

I had no mother to talk to me, or for me to ask questions, and both my husband and myself being of a reserved nature, I suffered, perhaps, more than I need have done. I needed chloroform and instruments in each case, and after the birth of my second child, I was a cripple for nearly twelve months, but having a good husband, I tried to bear patiently. I cannot say much else, except that now I can call it mock modesty on my part.

Wages 28s. to 36s.; three children, one still-born.

46. A healthy mill-worker.

I myself have had five children, all living. I had the five in seven years and two months, so you see for yourself I had them all very little, and no Maternity benefit to help me, and only a small wage coming in – say 25s. a week – so I had to go back to the mill when fit for work, to help to keep home right, which I don't think did me or the children any harm, for I have not paid 10s. to a doctor in all the bringing up of the five children, nor for myself. No still-born nor any miscarriages.

Wages 25s.; five children.

47. 'I think a lot.'

Oh, for the time when the Maternity Scheme becomes law, and the Divorce Reform. No one will welcome it more than I, for the sake of those who have not got true companionship in life. I am afraid I cannot tell you much about myself during pregnancy, as I have only had one child and no miscarriage. Perhaps my husband and myself have taken a different view from most people. You see, we both belong to a large family of brothers and sisters, and both had a drunken father, who did not care for their wife and offspring as much as the beast of the field.

My mother, whom I loved with all my heart, brought fifteen little lives into the world; twelve are still living. I remember many a time she has gone without food before and after confinement, and without fire in winter. I have gone round the house many a time to try and find a few rags to sell for food. I have seen my father strike my mother just before confinement, and known her be up again at four days' end to look after us. You see, my mother had no education, and had been brought up to obey her husband. But, poor dear, she left the cares of this world some years ago now, at the age of fifty-nine. My father has always been in business for himself, and used to have plenty of money, but spent it on himself, and is still living at the age of seventy-four. When I got married to the man I loved, and who loves me, he said I should never suffer as our dear mothers had done, and that we would only have what little lives we could make happy, and give a chance in life. My son will be eighteen years of age in June, and is still at Technical College, for which he won a scholarship. I get no grant-in-aid, and my husband is only a working man, so I go out to work for two hours every morning to help to keep him, as he is a good lad.

Please excuse my ramble, as I only wish I was better educated. I think a lot, but cannot express it, as I had to leave school at the age of ten years, to go into farm service. I have found the Guild a great help.

Wages 26s.; one child.

48. 'A time of horror.'

My two last babies came to me in troublous times, the boy, four years since, when my husband (through being too prosperous and false friends) gave way to drink, although he never tried to strike me, or any of the outward cruelty that I know many wives have to contend with; but it was so different to what I had been used to, and three months before the baby came, I was practically an invalid. Up till dinner I could manage to get about, but after dinner I had to lie or sit as best I could. I could not get on nine in men's shoes, my feet swelled up so, and every night my hands were in agonies; the only relief I got was when I used to hammer them on the wall, to try and take the awful dumb pain out of them. Then when I started in labour, I was in it from eleven o'clock on the night of Thursday, the 17th of February till Saturday, the 19th, at 10 a.m. The waters broke at eleven o'clock on Thursday night, and baby came at ten o'clock on Saturday. The doctor had to put it back, as it was not coming naturally. Of course, I had chloroform; indeed, I had it with all my seven children, except two, as I have always such long and terrible labours, although I am a big woman – 5 feet 8 inches, and I weigh over 13½ stone. I flooded with two. By the way, I am never able to get up under three weeks after confine-ment, as I always start to flood directly I make any movement, and I have to keep my nurse from five to seven weeks after. I always have terribly sore breasts, although the doctor treats them three months before-hand, but it makes no difference. My last confinement was worst, as I found, five months before baby was born, that my husband was having an immoral going-on. The shock was so great, I could not speak when first I heard it. A cold shiver went over me, and my body seemed to go together in a hard lump. I was never right after, till she came. Indeed, I was never right till my operation last October. I always had a weary bearing-down pain in my body all the time I was carrying babies, and suffer a great deal in my back. I never had morning sickness with any of them, and not one varicose vein, I am so thankful to say. And yet I know many women who can go right up to a few hours before, and then tell me they think nothing about it, while to me it is like a time of horror from beginning to end. I suppose we are differently made, somehow.

My husband earned 6d. an hour, and some of the summer months he worked overtime at the same rate of wages. What he earned overtime we always put in the Post Office, and what else we could spare towards the long winter months, as many times we started short time in August, which did not bring in very much. Then we were very lucky if we were getting 10s. a week at Christmas-time, but it used to be oftener *nothing* for weeks before Christmas. But we never went into debt. What we could not pay for we did without, and I can assure you I have told my husband many times that I had had my dinner before he came in, so as there should be plenty to go round for the children and himself, but he found me out somehow, and so that was stopped, although I had been many times only half filled, and I am glad to say during the worst of the pinch time I was not pregnant.

Seven children and three miscarriages.

49. Very hard times.

I seem to have had a very hard time all through. Well, my first baby was born twenty-three years last February, and my husband was working just about one or two days in a week at 3s. 4d. a day. My second baby was born sixteen months after, being still-born. My husband was out of work for three months then. I did nothing but cry. I could not get what I ought to have. The doctor wanted to know if I had been in any trouble. My mother told him how long we had been out of work, and I had cried a good deal. The doctor said that would be the cause of my baby being dead. When I got better, I went to work (and to tell you the truth, I have worked hard ever since). Twelve months after that I had another baby. I was very ill. When I got better, I took in plain sewing; then two years after I had another baby, but my husband was in better employment, earning 18s. per week, and I thought I was a lady. But it was not for long. My husband's work finished, and we moved to ——, where I had fresh troubles, my next baby being dead born, and my next only lived five months. When I was laid up again we were very hard up. I had to let the young person who looked after me go before her time was up. After I paid her and my rent and coals we had no dinner the Sunday, simply because we could not afford any. I always tried to get on and keep us all respectable, but it was hard work. I also managed to get the doctor paid before I wanted him again. Two and a half years after I had another baby, and she has taken more to rear her than all the rest; she cannot go to school. She takes such a lot of fits, both night and day. My next baby was born about eighteen months after, and when she was five I had the misfortune to go to bed again; I had a very bad time, although it was my tenth child. I was chloroformed, and the baby lived half an hour. I am sure you will be tired reading all my troubles, but I assure you I had to work hard in my home and out of it to keep us all together. I used to buy extra every week, it did not matter how small, so that I could be better able to pay for someone to look after me. I have a good husband, and he helps me all he can. Three of my daughters is under the doctor now, and I am of the candid opinion it is through me working so hard and not getting plenty of food and attention during that period. I hope I have not wearied you. I many a time feel I could write a book of my troubles; I seem to have had so many. When we look back, we wonder however we have got along, but every cloud has a silver lining, and I am looking forward to see my children better provided than I have been. With all good wishes for a brighter future.

Wages 18s. to 22s.; eight children, two still-births.

50. A farm-worker's wife.

I have had four children; the oldest is now twenty-three, the next twenty-two, the next twenty-one, and the youngest fourteen. I might say that at the time my three eldest were born, my husband was working on a farm, and earning 18s. a week. When the last was born he had moved into rather better work, and earned 25s. a week. You may be sure after I had paid 3s. for a small cottage of two rooms and scullery, I had not much to spare, and of course doctors had to be paid. As for nursing, well, I did not get much of it, and I feel very deeply always the need of good nursing at these times. For years I suffered from what I feel was the want of proper nursing and nourishment. In fact I wonder sometimes even now if I have ever really got over it. When I think of it I feel I would do anything to support any measure that would help to secure that our daughters now shall not suffer as their mothers did before them.

Wages 18s. to 25s.; four children.

51. Shun patent foods.

As you will see (from my having lost six children in succession before I reared one), I was very unfortunate in my early married life, and at one time thought I was not going to rear any children. Congenital weakness may have had something to do with the failure to rear, through falling down a flight of stairs as a girl and dislocating my neck. This fall would have cost me my life but for the presence of mind of a young woman who picked me up. Using her hands and knees, she pulled my neck in, and undoubtedly saved my life. The doctor said I would suffer as a woman, for every organ internally was put out of place. My first set of children were weakly, and being unable to nurse them, I resorted to patent foods, which I am now firmly convinced did harm and not good, and in my opinion contributed to the convulsions. I found later that weakened milk, afterwards strengthened as the baby got older, was the best and safest food for infants brought up by hand. Undoubtedly the remaining ones progressed all right, and are sound and healthy. The fact that one girl put ten and a half years' perfect attendance in at an elementary school speaks well for the change. The one I lost at seven weeks was easily accounted for, from the fact that at the time of birth I was suffering from the bloody flux, a very severe form of dysentery. In fact, the doctor said that if I had had Asiatic cholera I could not have been worse. You will readily see that that child had a very poor start in life, and waned away from birth. As a result of my experience, my advice is that mothers unable to suckle their children should shun all patent foods, rusks, etc., as they would shun the devil himself, for an infant will have to be born with a digestion like a horse if it is to digest solid food in the early stages. Thousands of infants are killed with mistaken kindness, and I am convinced that milk and milk only – human, if possible, and animal, if human fails – in a diluted state, is the only safe food for infants. I sincerely hope you will sound a note of warning against patent foods that cake to a solid lump in the infant's stomach, the result being convulsions and death. This is my sincere belief resulting from bitter experience.

Wages 24s. to 30s.; ten children.

52. 'Get very little pity.'

I am the mother of a large family, but I am glad to say they are fast growing up, as their ages range from twenty-eight down to five years, so that I feel I can speak from experience, if anyone can. I must say that although it is a time that women suffer terribly, yet it is a time when they get very little pity, as it is looked upon as quite a natural state of things. I have myself got up in the morning, unable to partake of any breakfast, and tried to get about my work, and had to sit down in every chair I have got to with my brush in my hand. Then after confinement, as soon as I could sit up in bed, having such a large family, I have had to sit with my needle in my hand. But all this does no good, but only tends to keep a woman's health down. When I had my first miscarriage – it happened in October – and I crawled about all the winter, and well on into the next summer, like a person in consumption; in fact, it was generally thought that I was. And, of course, all those months we were obliged to have a woman in, as I could do nothing. So I think if anything could be done to lessen the sufferings of the coming generations, I for one should be in great favour of it, as of course, if it is too late for me to benefit by it, I have daughters growing up, and sons' wives to think of. Suffering as I have done, it is really a time when extra funds are needed, so that one could pay a little to have anything done, instead of having to do it themselves.

Wages 17s. 8d.; nine children, six miscarriages.

53. Work in the mill.

When I have been pregnant I have suffered very much with bad legs. You see, I had to go to work in the mill, and so I had not the chance to give them the rest they needed. I think it is a great hardship for a woman to have to do so. However, when I have got over the confinement, I seemed to pull up after my first baby. But after my second one was born I was in bed nearly a month, and my husband (who, thank God, is one of the best) had to lift me in and out of bed, and put my legs on a level with my body while he made my bed. After the third I was something the same, only not quite so bad.

My babies have been very strong and healthy, though they have not always had the best of health since. But I have tried to do my duty to them as well as I could.

I might say that I think ignorance has more to do with suffering than anything, and I think if our Guilds would get the doctors to lecture to them on this subject it might help our members, and also other people, to take more care of themselves.

Three children.

54. In favour of breast-feeding.

I have not had children as fast as some, for which I am thankful, not because I do not love them, but because if I had more I do not think I could have done my duty to them under the circumstances. I may say I have had a very good partner in life, and that has made it better for me. But seeing my husband is only a weaver, I have not had a lot of money to go on with. I have been compelled to go out to work. I have worked when I have been pregnant, but I have always given up when I have been about six months, and then I have done all my own work up to the very last, and I can tell you it has been very hard work. Then when it has been over I have had to begin to do my housework at the fortnight end, and I think that is too soon, but what can women do when they have not the means to do it with? Of course, I am not half so bad as some. I have never carried a baby out to nurse. I have always managed to stop at home one year and get them walking. But I think if we as women had our right, we should not have to work at all during pregnancy, because I think that both the mother and baby would be better. I never knew so many bottle-fed babies as there is now. Nearly all the young married women cannot give breast. How is it? Now, I think because they work so hard before, do not get enough rest, therefore have no milk. And, then, some will not begin with their own milk, because they know they have to go out to work. Hence the baby has to suffer. Mother's milk is the best food for baby. I heard a young mother with her first baby say the other day her husband's mother had told her not to bother with her breasts, it made a young woman look old giving her baby breast. What a mother! I think it is one of the grandest sights to see. So you see we have a lot of educating to do yet when we hear such things as these.

Wages 16s. to 30s.; four children.

55. Mixed experiences.

I have three girls. Over my first child the only ailments I had were sickness during the first five months, and at childbirth I had a very good time. And over the second a much similar time, with the exception of colds in my face. Over my third baby I had a much harder time, as during the whole of the nine months I was unable to do anything, as I had such terrible pains in my back and legs – could not bear to be on my feet for more than a few minutes at a time.

During all this illness of mine I had my husband at home ill sixteen weeks, which of course made it worse for me, as the extra worry went against me; and then at the same time I had an abscess in my breast, which I can assure you was most painful, as I can tell you I had my hands pretty well full at that time.

Wages 14s. to £2; three children.

56. Twelve children.

I have had a large family (twelve) and a miscarriage. I had a hard struggle at the beginning, my husband not being in very good work. But for the last five children I was able to pay for someone to wash, and that made a lot of difference.

But as far as the confinement went, I always had pretty fair times, and got up fairly well.

I have had two bad attacks of the heart since I had the last child, which is six years old, and the doctor told me it was with having so many children, and so quick. But I am getting better. And the doctor said I should get better if nothing else happened.

Wages £1; twelve children, one miscarriage.

57. Dreadful sufferings.

In my case all my pregnancy times have been rather bad. Had I been less fortunate in finding a good husband, and one who was able to keep at home, one thinks, I should never have been living today. I have cost pounds and pounds besides the care and anxiety in bringing my two into the world. My first was a miscarriage owing to a fall while hanging a picture. Was in bed over a fortnight, and almost drained bloodless. My second, a fine bouncing girl – unfortunately too fine. I had to be stitched twice, the first at confinement, the second three weeks later, caused by the agony of a gathered breast. I was eight weeks ill at that time. My third, I could scarcely walk about for six weeks before confinement owing to strain on weak parts, and only short of eighteen months of previous confinement. I had to be stitched again, but managed to ward off the breast trouble to a great extent; incapable for five weeks. My last was the worst; we had removed away to a strange place, and I happened to get a woman who did not know her work. I was very ill at the time, but everything was favourable until the third day I developed childbed fever. I went blind, sometimes unconscious, my breasts in slings, so large I could not see over the top, inflammation of the bowels, and blood-poisoning; I was almost beyond hope, and was seriously ill three weeks. Then took a turn for the better. We had to get a thoroughly efficient person in, the cost of which was £1 per week for seven weeks, and, God bless her, she deserved every farthing she got, although it was hard. We had to pay again for other housework to be done. I feel I owe much of my recovery to her. My husband was seriously reduced in means, but he would have sold anything to do good. When I got sufficiently well I had to go to hospital; was a patient there a month, was fetched home, carried to bed, and stayed there six weeks, owing to abscesses from the stitching being delayed so long and bad condition of my system. I am not a strong person now, but I am now in my forty-sixth year, and seem to be improving in a good many respects.

The highest wage my husband earned was 45s., the lowest, and at the worst time, being £1 – just the amount the nurse required, besides all else – washing, cooking food, and everything a home needs.

Wages 20s. to 45s.; three children, one miscarriage.

58. Inefficient doctor.

My first baby was born fifteen months after marriage. During the first four or five months I suffered very much from sickness, not morning sickness only, but many times during the whole day, and nearly all the way through severe toothache … As a result of inattention by the doctor attending me I was badly torn during the birth, and after three days my husband dismissed him and called in another doctor, who said though this could not always be avoided it might have been in my case. I ought to have been stitched at the time, instead of which it was done four days after.

It was four years and six months later when my second

baby came. I was much better during pregnancy – occasional morning sickness. There was the fear all through of the tear reopening, but with having a good period between the births the parts were strong enough to resist, and all went well. Six years afterwards, I had a miscarriage about three months. Don't know how to account for it, excepting that there is so little rest in the married working woman's life. From early morning until late at night she is on her feet. I was more fortunately placed than most women; I was able to go to bed and be attended to, and to stay there until I was better.

Four years after my third baby was born (still-born). This was the worst time I had, the sickness being most distressing, so bad that could not describe it, and one was always afraid of a miscarriage owing to everything being forced down through straining. At these times it was impossible to hold one's water. At seven months, as a result of this bearing-down, I had a flooding bout, and was in bed several days. I had no labour pains, though weak and poorly, and so did not send for the doctor. I know now that I ought to have done so at once, as my life was in danger. However, I got up again and did my ordinary duties until the day of the birth, which was harder than usual, as a live baby helps in its own way. The baby had gradually died after the flooding, and had been dead more than a week at birth. I was in a very low condition for the first three days, the doctor being uncertain how things would go. There is always the danger of blood-poisoning, and it takes one much longer to get their health back in cases of this kind. Where there is a large family or a thoughtless husband the woman pays with her life.

Wages 25s. to £2; two children, one still-birth, one miscarriage.

59. Household help needed.

I may say that during pregnancy I suffered considerably the whole time from sickness and severe pains. This was not due to any traceable cause, as I took every precaution to see that I did not exert myself and do harm. I did all my own work all the while. I had little appetite, and was not able to sleep well. During confinement I had a very hard time, and was a long time in recovering, and have always, since my first child, suffered from falling of the womb, although I had a doctor and midwife in the house three weeks. It is owing to working women having to take on household duties too soon after confinement that is responsible for the greatest part of the sufferings which we are subject to. What is really wanted is a supply of real good midwives who could be got for a month to see to all requirements of the patient and the home while the woman has a fair chance of recovering. It is the system of midwives attending too many cases at the same time that is responsible for a lot of the trouble, as the woman gets neglected and are forced to get about before they are fit.

Wages 30s. to 35s.; three children, one still-born.

60. Miscarriages.

After my first little one I went out too soon, with the result that I got cold in the ovaries, which caused me the most acute pain, and for quite a month every few steps I walked I would sit down. I have had several miscarriages – one caused through carelessness in jumping up to take some clothes off the line when it commenced to rain, instead of getting a chair to stand on, another through taking some pills which were delivered as samples at the door, and a third through a fright by a cow whilst on holidays. So you will see I realise to the full the care and thought a woman requires. I may say that to me the after-effects of the miscarriages have been worse than confinements, for it takes months to get over the weakness.

Wages 26s. to 30s.; two children, three miscarriages.

61. A very sad case.

The man and woman I know, who are very steady people, have six children. The three elder ones are quite normal. After the birth of the third the father had a very serious illness – double pneumonia followed by typhoid fever – and for weeks he lay at death's door. The expense of all this so reduced them that they had to sell the best of their furniture to pay doctor's bills, over £20, and to keep going until he could start work again. Then the doctor said he must not go back to his work as a mason, and he had to take a job at labouring work. This and short time brought his income down to 14s. per week, and to make ends meet the wife had to go out cleaning. She had been parlourmaid. She continued to do so until near the birth of her fourth child, who was very delicate and suffered from abscesses. The mother told me she did not know how to get sufficient food for them. When her fifth child was born she had a bad time and the child appeared very backward, but it was not until it was two years old that they knew its brain was affected. He is in his sixth year, and can only say a few words, and has never come downstairs, always had to be carried, and at times is violent; if thwarted in what he wants to do will go into violent tempers and throw anything he may have in his hand. He will also put a rope round the neck of the younger child to play horses, and has no control over bowels. A sad case indeed. The youngest child is in his fourth year, and can only walk two or three yards without help. He cannot say a word yet. I am beginning to be afraid he may be dumb. Both his hands are deformed, and he has no control over bowels, and has been ruptured from birth. Doctors say they cannot perform any operation until he is stronger. When the mother asked the doctor how it was her children were so delicate, he turned to her and said in the kindest possible manner, 'Ask the mother,' showing that it was due, in his opinion, to the weak state she was in previous to their birth. I do not think the two youngest will ever be able to work for themselves. The mother looks almost distracted at times. I have known her from girlhood, and pity her most sincerely.

Six children.

62. State maternity homes wanted.

My husband is a non-smoker and total abstainer, so you will know no money was spent in waste. But I feel sure my first baby was still-born through hard work and lifting. The money brought in not being sufficient to keep us all, I went out to work, and looked after my husband and step-children as well.

I feel sure it is not so much lack of knowledge as lack of means that entails so much suffering. I endured agonies when carrying my second child, through bad varicose veins in legs and body, but of course still had to plod on and look after the rest. I had knowledge of what to eat to produce milk, etc., but could only confine myself to cocoa and oatmeal, which I often felt sick at the sight of, but could afford nothing else, as I made these things for the rest of the family also. I at the second confinement produced a fine boy, 9½ pounds in weight. He is now eight, and is still a very fine boy. The medical officer, when examining him, passed a very pointed remark, saying: 'He is, of course, an only child,' and I often feel thankful he is. We live in quite a poor house, 7s. 6d. weekly rent, but to do justice to my grown-up step-children, so that they may live up to standard required of by their work, I cannot afford to have any more children, also I cannot face the awful agonies a woman has to go through in looking after a family (there are five of us in the home now) whilst child-bearing. When I had my boy I had to do the family washing in the third week after confinement. As to taking care, no working woman can do that unless absolutely obliged to. The best thing that could happen would be a system of State Maternity Homes, where working women could go for a reasonable fee and be confined, and stay for convalescence (not a workhouse system). There is no peace for the wife at home. She is still the head and chancellor of the exchequer. If she were confined on Friday, she would still have to plan and lay out the Saturday money, and if it did not stretch far enough, she would be the one to go short or do the worrying. I am sure if we, as a Guild, could bring this about, a lot of women's worry would be over. At the same time it would be a recognition of the importance of our women as race-bearers, and lift her to a higher plane than at present.

My husband's highest wages during the time you ask were 36s., lowest 24s., but in his trade wet weather and frosty weather means no work, and in addition no pay during slack times.

There is one thing – as to mechanical prevention of family. I know it is a delicate subject, but it is an urgent one, as it is due to low-paid wages and the unearthly struggle to live respectably. All the beautiful in motherhood is very nice if one has plenty to bring up a family on, but what real mother is going to bring a life into the world to be pushed into the drudgery of the world at the earliest possible moment because of the strain on the family exchequer.

I was much struck with the remarks of 'Kitchener's' boys who have been billeted on me, about my boy. He is only nine, and they said he was as big as the general run of lads in the North when they are thirteen – 'But then, ma, you've only one to keep, which is different to seven or eight.'

There is nothing that is done can ever be too much if we are to have going a race in the future worthy of England, but it will not be until the nation wakes up to the needs of the mothers of that future race.

Wages 24s. to 36s.; one child, one still-birth,
one miscarriage.

63. 'A miserable experience.'

I am really not a delicate woman, but having a large family, and so fast, pulled me down very much. I used to suffer very much with bad legs; and my husband was laid out of work most winters, so I had a great deal of poverty to deal with.

Nearly all my children were delicate, and being badly off, very often I could not get or do what I would like to for them. I lost four out of the ten, and had a very great difficulty in rearing some of the others. They were nearly all two years before they ran; my eldest girl was three years before she ran; I never thought she could live, but, thank God, she has lived, and is nearly twenty-two. If something could be done for poor women with large families, I think it would be a good thing; for a woman's life is not much when she is in poverty and got sickly children, and never knows what an hour's liberty is. It is keep on work with no rest days, and not much nights very often. Of course, during pregnancy one never feels well, what with one thing and the other. That was my experience; and after confinement I used to be so weak, and by the time I began to regain my strength a little I was in trouble again. So you can't wonder poor delicate women break down and very often die. It would be good if something could be done for them, so as to give them a change and a little rest. And when you have got an unkind husband it is a terrible life. I very often think that is why my poor children have to suffer so much now they are grown up, as they are not any of them strong, and very often ailing with one thing or the other. You may depend on it there is a good many women got unkind husbands that make it a great deal worse for women.

My husband used to lose his work through drink. I couldn't tell you exactly what my wages were, but I feel almost sure, to take the years through, they never amounted to £1 a week. I was in hopes, as soon as my boys started work, I should have got on better, but the more I got off my boys the less I got off my husband, for mine has been a miserable experience.

For a good many years I kept account of what he gave me, and to take the year through it used to amount to about 15s. a week.

Wages unknown, wife's allowance 15s. to £1; ten children, two miscarriages.

64. 'Best of times are bad.'

I have been most fortunate, and have had very good times, so they tell me, but the best of times are bad enough. I have had four healthy children, and had them all before I was twenty-seven years of age.

Wages 26s.; four children.

65. Every attention.

During the whole time I was pregnant I had every care and attention, and a good doctor and nurse at my confinement.

Wages 25s.; one child.

66. Very good health.

I am by nature very active, and during pregnancy had very good health, and was able to look after my home and family up to the time of confinement. My confinements have not been what would be called bad times.

Wages 30s. to 36s.; four children.

67. 'A steady and regular income.'

Having fairly good health, my experiences were only the perfectly natural ones, though at the time I thought it was hard to bear. I was fortunate enough to have a steady and regular income, and consequently put myself in my doctor's hands at the earliest possible moment, and had all the care and nursing that is every woman's right to have.

Two children.

68. 'Read, studied, and took care.'

I am not, nor have ever been, a very robust woman, so naturally felt the strain of pregnancy perhaps more than some women feel it, but coming away from home as I did, over two hundred miles, when I was married, when I found out my condition, I put myself in the hands of a good doctor, and that helped me a good deal.

With neither of my children was I troubled with sickness, but was troubled a great deal with inflammation and heartburn, with which I had to be very careful, and it prevented me getting about much, especially the last three months. I had splendid times at confinement, but have not been able to nurse either of my children. I tried for four months with the last one, but the baby did not get on, and myself came down very low. I was obliged to resort to artificial feeding, and the baby never looked back after. I do not think any of my troubles came at these times through ignorance. I am one that has always taken great interest in these subjects, and read and studied all I could about them, and naturally took great care of myself at these times. But having at all times weak digestive organs, the extra strain on them during pregnancy brought forth the troubles I had to fight with both before and after confinement.

I do not think any women expect to go through these times without some small amount of – shall I say? – trouble, for which she is fully recompensed when she can take her dear child in her arms.

Wages 45s. to 47s.; two children.

69. Preventives.

I was married before I was twenty, and eleven months afterwards my first baby was born. During pregnancy I suffered dreadfully from nervousness, very bad legs, occasional neuralgia, and the usual miserable sickness. Indeed, before baby came I felt very bad indeed.

I had a stiff but quite straightforward confinement. My husband worked on the water, and only came home once a week, or how I could have shown a cheerful face every day, and got through my work, I don't know.

For some months after baby was born I was weak and ill. I nursed her myself, and when she was a year old, I weaned her. When she was a year and nine months old, my second baby was born. I had been through the usual sickness, bad legs, neuralgia, etc., but I had a good confinement. I hoped to get up well; but I can assure you I had the most miserable six months of my life. No physical pain, but extreme weakness, frightened of my own shadow, faintings, feelings that I would die. Indeed, I was almost tired of life. I had continually to go to bed, my head felt a tremendous size, and I felt as though I were floating away.

When this baby was two years and three months old, my first boy was born; I had had a miserable nine months, legs worse than ever, bad cough, sickness, etc., but a good time.

After this, I said to a friend one day, 'If only I could feel that this was my last, I would be quite happy.' 'Well,' she said, 'why don't you make it your last?' and she gave me advice.

As a result of this knowledge, I had no more babies for four and a half years. In carrying this one, I certainly had the bad legs, which I am likely to keep, but my general health and nerves were much better. My health improved, and people said I looked years younger, and I found life a happy place. I sometimes think that the Great Almighty has heard the poor woman in travail, and shows her a way of rest. I had a fight with my conscience before using a preventative. But I have no qualms now. I feel I have better health to serve my husband and children, and more advantages to give them; while if another comes along, we will hail it with pleasure, as we did our last, instead of looking on it as a burden.

I do think that a great deal of misery is caused by taking drugs. The poor woman feels she will do anything to keep herself 'all right.' If only she and her husband also could be taught how to prevent, much good might be done.

I had never resorted to drugs; I was just a simple girl, and my young husband was as simple as myself.

I often feel, too, how hard it is that when a woman is carrying and needs extra nourishment and rest she has to stint herself, to provide for the expensive time coming, or try and add to her household linen by taking in work, or taking lodgers or boarders.

Wages 30s. to 35s.; four children.

70. The teaching of experience.

I am in fairly comfortable circumstances for a working-class woman, and have a good, considerate husband. I have had six children. You will see by the enclosed particulars that there is not much difference between the ages of my first three children – as a matter of fact, not nearly enough – and this through ignorance. At the birth of my second child 'flooding' occurred, leaving me very anaemic as a consequence. I could not nurse the child, and was an out-patient at the hospital for five months.

Then I became pregnant with third child, and at the seventh month a miscarriage was threatened, but was averted for a few weeks, when the baby was born an eight-months child. It was a delicate child, and required a great deal of care and attention; although ailing myself for months, I managed to rear him to a fairly healthy child, but, oh, it was such a strain!

I am so glad the Guild is taking up the question of Maternity, and also 'Moral Hygiene,' as I feel sure if only young people were advised, both before and after marriage – a great deal of suffering caused to mother and child might be avoided.

My husband and I are quite determined not to allow any of our children to marry without first explaining to them the great responsibilities of creating a new life that is to be pure and healthy.

Wages 30s.; six children.

71. 'But it is too late.'

I am sending you my experiences as near as I can. I was married at twenty-one years. I am now forty-five. I have had no children this last eight years. I can safely say I am suffering now for my ignorance in my young days, during pregnancy and confinement. It was after my second baby was born; I was living a piece away from my mother. I could not afford to pay someone to look after the house and me, and pay a midwife too, so my mother came and did what she could for me in the morning, and then left me till my husband came from work. Of course, I got up sooner than I should have done. It was in January, and snow was about. I went in the back place, and started to put things right, when I had a cold shake, and I was put to bed. It stopped all the courses, and I was many weeks before I was right. Since then I have suffered with varicose veins in my legs before and after confinement.

I have been in bed four and five weeks, the longest nine weeks, with my legs, after baby was born. At the present time of writing I am in bed now, and have been nearly three weeks with the same thing. Now the change has come. It is three years since I had an attack.

I think I was getting about 26s. off my husband.

Thank God, my husband has been very good in all my sickness. If he had not, I could not have lived through it. I feel sure I should not be suffering now, if I could have had money to pay to be looked after then. Of course, I am better off now, but it is too late.

Wife's allowance 26s.; nine children and one miscarriage.

72. Loss of strength.

I was married at the age of nineteen years. My boy was born when I was twenty-one years. Although during pregnancy I realised I was to become a mother, I had never been taught what I should do or should not do during that time. One of my sufferings during pregnancy was due to over-sensitiveness. I have thought, especially since hearing Mrs. ——'s address on 'Moral Hygiene,' what a comfort and help it would have been to me, had the above subject been taught when we were young by school-teachers, or had our mothers realised the need of explaining nature as a necessary form of education. I do hope that the community will soon realise how necessary it is for boys and girls to have knowledge of this important subject.

When I was confined, the doctor and monthly nurse were both with me. A few hours after the birth of my boy, when the nurse brought me some gruel, I sat up in bed to eat, but was soon told to lie down again. I do not know whether it was due to that act of ignorance, but I suffered with my back for a long time. My boy when born was a big and lovely baby; he is now eleven years old, a picture of health, standing 5 feet and ½ inch in his stockings.

I felt very well while lying in bed after my boy was born. It was when I got up and dressed the tenth day I realised my weakness. I was glad to lie on my back in less than an hour after.

My husband had been out of work for six weeks during the time of pregnancy, and again another six weeks when baby was four and a half months old. I have mentioned the above fact, for I am sure it was partly due to that that I did not regain my strength for years after. I fed the baby on the breast for thirteen months. By that time I felt so low that it was an effort to walk upstairs, and was glad to sit on the top stair to pull myself together; so I went on until I got really ill. I was under the doctor's care for three months. Meanwhile I had had several attacks of inflammation inwardly, but the last attack was so severe I myself was frightened. The doctor then told me it would be some time before I regained my strength. I certainly gained strength after that illness; part of it, I feel, was due to rest.

Wages 21s. to 31s. 6d.; one child.

73. Suffering and hard work.

During the early stages of pregnancy, with first baby, I was very much subject to a fainting condition, which I was informed was a perfectly natural condition during such a period, and could not be avoided. Whether such be the case or not, I cannot say. Otherwise my health generally was very good, being at that particular time blessed with an excellent robust constitution. My first baby was one year and eleven months old when the second one arrived. During the first four months of pregnancy with second child, except suffering violently from morning sickness (another thing I am told cannot be dispensed with), I maintained my usual state of health. After four months had elapsed a pain developed in my right side (I can compare it only to a gnawing toothache), which caused me a great deal of annoyance through the day, and most restless nights. This continued until my baby was born. I recovered splendidly from my confinement, but owing to circumstances had to be about performing household duties much earlier than I ought to have been. My third baby was born two years and eight months after second one. Whilst carrying this baby, from very early stage, I was distracted with an almost unbearable itching in the exterior part of the abdomen. In fact, I thought I should have gone mad with it, and had I then had the means at my disposal to consult my medical adviser (but 2s. 6d. was a great consideration to me at that time, for one visit, out of a small income), I could have been spared a great amount of agony ... During pregnancy with my third and fourth babies, I had to contend with the pain in my side, as with the second one. I attribute this pain to having to carry one child about so much whilst in a state of pregnancy with another, and not being able to employ anyone to assist me in the more laborious duties, such as washing, scrubbing, etc., to give me the necessary rest which my condition demanded. When my third baby arrived, I regret to say it was disfigured with a hare-lip, from which cause it could not take its food properly, which caused it to cry almost incessantly, and after a trying period of eleven weeks, she, poor little mite, succumbed. Owing to the worry connected with this misfortune, also having to be up again too soon after confinement, and for want of rest, I felt my health giving way, and being in a weak condition, I became an easy prey to sexual intercourse, and thus once more I became a mother in fourteen months. My health was very moderate whilst in pregnancy with my fourth and last baby, now seven years of age, which I attribute solely to having children too quickly in succession, and in not procuring, as I said before, the necessary rest and nourishment which is essential to a mother at these periods.

Since the birth of my last child I have suffered from a falling womb, which my doctor informs me has been caused by getting out of bed too soon after confinements, which was due entirely to not having the wherewithal to provide for adequate attention.

I feel very keen concerning this problem, and do hope something will be done in the very near future to alleviate the unnecessary suffering of working mothers.

During the time I was having my children, my husband's

average weekly earnings were 25s. When working over-time he may have earned 30s. or even 32s., but on the other hand, when on short time or holidays (which are equivalent to short time – no work, no pay), I have known him to receive as low as 15s. or 12s. To give you an instance. Christmas week of last year his wages amounted to 12s., and New Year week this year, 10s. My husband, along with myself, considered his wages were not adequate to maintain a family, provide proper attention, etc., during confinement, and solely for this reason we do not feel jus-tified in having any more children if it can possibly be avoided. I love children dearly, another reason why I do not wish to create them to be badly fed, clothed badly, uneducated, etc., on a mere pittance. I could say much more, but my sincere desire is that a better time is dawn-ing for working-class mothers and their babies.

Wages 15s. to 32s.; four children.

74. 'Heavy wash-days.'

I think a great deal of suffering might be spared, especially over the first child, if the mother could only have had a little more knowledge how to go on, *re* the suffering. I have been prostrated for days with violent sickness and pain in the head. The case of miscarriage was a very bad one, resulting in having to attend the hospital nearly two years. The doctor says the miscarriage was caused by heavy wash-days, one of the things I think the expectant mother ought not to have to do; but it is one of the most important things in the home. I think if the mother could only be allowed to take care of herself the first three months of the time, many both deformed and deficient children might be avoided. I do not mean for a mother to lead an idle life for three months, because exercise is most necessary in a proper way; but such work as washing, paper-hanging, whitewashing, and hanging clothes up to dry, is the work that has serious results with the mother. My results after confinement can, I think, be traced to the lack of good nursing and good support – in such cases when one neighbour will nurse another one, having had no experience herself.

Wages 28s. 3d. to 37s. 6d.; five children, one miscarriage.

75. Bad effects of hard work.

I think your Maternity Scheme just splendid. You will see by accompanying form I have lost two of my four babies, and had a miscarriage. If I had taken more care before birth, I quite believe those children would have lived.

I have always had good health, and quite able to do my work up to the last, but I think now it is quite wrong for the mother to try to do *hard* work a month or six weeks before or after. That means she wants three months real care.

In my case before those two were born, I had to work harder than usual, and the consequences were they were born delicate.

My two children that I have reared are strong and healthy, and I had no troubles or worries or hard work before they were born. I could also take things easy until they were six weeks old.

There is one other point; the mother who works and worries generally loses the milk which is so necessary for the baby. If only mothers could take it easy during that time, I am certain we could rear a much better race. I often feel I shall be able to help my own daughter, should she need it, for the mothers of the past were ignorant.

Wages 26s. to 32s.; four children, one miscarriage.

76. Amongst strangers.

I think many of us have suffered (and do so now) through lack of care during pregnancy, especially over a first child. If something could be done to help the expectant mother to understand how best to care for herself, then much suffering would be saved afterwards.

I went to live many miles away from my home and friends when I married, amongst strangers, and was too shy to ask anyone what I should or should not do (when I knew I should become a mother), and was so ill, tired, and depressed that I felt I did not want to do anything. A dear old woman, one of the neighbours, came to me one day, and asked me if I had been to a doctor; I said 'No; I was going to speak to one nearer the time.' She said, 'My dear girl; go to him now. Tell him how you are. I am sure he will be able to give you something to ease that excessive sickness, etc., and advise you how best to take care of yourself.'

I did not go to him for some time, but eventually did so, and felt much better for his advice and care during that trying time.

I had rather hard times at the birth of my little ones, and can quite realise that it is most necessary that a woman should have the greatest care and attention possible. Still, I feel that if more could be done to teach them how to care for their own health before the birth of the little ones we should have healthier and stronger children. How it can be done without hurting the mothers' feelings is a very difficult problem, but I suffered so much before my first baby was born that perhaps I feel most strongly on the need of our sisters knowing how best to care for themselves. I am so glad the Maternity Scheme is being taken up so much more by Health Committees now since the Guild have worked for it.

Wages 25s. to 30s.; three children, one still-birth,
one miscarriage.

77. Care and attention.

I am afraid the information I can give you about myself is not much, as I have been able to have the care and attention not attainable for many working-women. My first baby was still-born. This was really brought about by ignorance during pregnancy in trying to open a very stiff window, causing a strain, and also causing the cord to become twisted round the baby's neck. Fortunately, I was able at once to receive medical attention, and when the child was born I had to have two doctors and nurse, chloroform, etc. Doctors both say I should have lost my life also if I had not had the attention I was able to have. The other two children were born under quite normal conditions – the symptoms of sickness, cholic pains, etc. – but I am glad to say I have never suffered from varicose veins, perhaps due to the fact that I have always been able to take rest during pregnancy.

My mother had thirteen children, and, as far as I can gather, suffered terribly at these times, because when a woman brings up ten children to full age she has not much time to rest. I may say one of hers was stillborn, the other two dying, one at the age of nine months from vaccination, the other at three years and a half from concussion of the brain.

Mother died at the age of fifty-two years from Bright's disease, brought on, I believe, from excessive child-bearing, and the doctor said every organ in her body was completely worn out. My mother had, perhaps, the care most women would not get, as my father was always in a good position earning a good salary – I may say £150 a year at that time. But with all those advantages, she could not have the care she ought, or the rest, and, of course, no trained nurses, as we have at the present time.

I often wonder when I read of the deaths of women, at from forty years of age upward, if, when they should be having the best of their lives, that their early deaths are due to lack of care and rest during the times they are having their babies.

78. Weakness following pregnancy.

I suffered very much in pregnancy, was violently sick quite a dozen times a day every day for the first six months, with occasional fainting attacks. I was better towards the end, but had bad nights, so had to rest a lot in the day. The baby was born all right, and I got on well, but was weak. When she was twelve months old (I nursed her myself) I had a goitre in my neck, which lasted two years. At one time I was very ill in hospital seven weeks, and away in country six. The doctor said it was weakness following pregnancy that caused it. I was not able to do my home duties, and if I had been a woman who had to go out to work – well, I could not have done so for nearly all the three years. My husband did not want any more children, as I suffered so much with the first. He is eleven years now, and I am very well.

Wages 30s.; one child.

79. Frequent pregnancies.

During pregnancy I was fairly well in health, but during my confinements I was very ill. I never had a natural birth ... I think what caused my miscarriages was with having children so quickly, and having to work rather hard at the same time.

Wife's allowance 24s.; five children and three miscarriages.

80. Husband on short time.

During pregnancy with my first child, after about three months, I started with inflammation of the bladder. I happened to be with my mother at the time, but had it been otherwise I could not have got anyone to look after me, as my husband was only working two and three days a week. Of course, my friends would have looked after me, but everyone is not so fortunate as that. I would have freely died, the pain was so severe. And whatever maternity benefit a wife and mother receives, she gets nothing more than she deserves, and I believe they will get the money as easy as they get the old age pensions, and they will have less to waste.

Wages 17s. 6d. to £2; three children.

81. Convulsions.

I very nearly lost my life over my first confinement, through being ignorant of how to take care of myself beforehand. I had lived about eighty miles away from home for some years, and was away from my mother at the time, also too shy and reticent to ever mention my condition to neighbours. I had always been strong and healthy, and never took medicine or aperients in any shape or form, in fact, never thought about it, and acted just the same when pregnant, although dreadfully constipated all the time. I thought it was a result of my condition. At confinement, after twenty-four hours' pain and suffering I was seized with convulsions just as the baby was at the point of being born, and knew no more for about twelve hours. Another doctor was fetched, and the child was got away somehow, also my friends telegraphed for, as they expected me to die. However, that did not happen. But the doctors said it was the only case of convulsions at confinement that they had ever heard of the patient living after, and they blamed it to the clogged condition of the bowels. I was quite normal over the second confinement. There may perhaps not be much in this, except, perhaps, if I had known a bit more about such things, it would have been a lot better for me. My girl is nineteen now.

It seems almost incredible that I was so ignorant, but I had lived quietly a long time with a strictly particular widow lady, and had hardly ever heard such things discussed.

Wages 10s. to 30s.; two children.

82. 'Every care on every occasion.'

I have eight children and one miscarriage from ptomaine poisoning. And never can I say I have not had every care on every occasion. My husband from the first saw that I had the necessary requirements. During the pregnancy of the last four I suffered from varicose veins, and there were days when I could not get about so well, but on the whole I am pleased to say I have always been able to do ordinary housework, with, of course, rests between.

After confinement, I always had the month out before commencing my house work, but I took the management of my baby as soon as possible, say from two weeks old.

I have all my children, never buried any.

Wages £2 to £3; eight children, one miscarriage.

83. A wage-earning mother.

I myself had some very hard times, as I had to go out to work in the mill. I was a weaver, and we had a lot of lifting to do. My first baby was born before its time, from me lifting my piece off the loom on to my shoulder, as two of us had them to lift, and then carry them from the shed across the yard to be weighed. If I had been able to take care of myself I should not have had to suffer as I did for seven weeks before that baby was born and for three months after; and then there was the baby suffering as well, as he was a weak little thing for a long time, and cost pounds that could have been saved had I been able to stay at home and look after myself. But I could not do so, as my husband was short of work; and when I had my second baby I had to work all through again, as my husband was short of work and ill at the time. So there was another poorly baby. While I was carrying this one he only worked three months out of the nine. I could not get any support at all then. I had to go out to work again at the month-end, and put the baby out to nurse. I had to get up by four in the morning, and get my baby out of bed, wash and dress it, and then leave home by five, as I had half an hour walk to take my baby to my mother's, and then go to my work and stand all day till half-past five at night, and then the walk home again with my baby. I had to do this with three of them. I think you will understand I have had my share; and all my children have had to be brought with instruments. I have had six living children and one mis-carriage. I lost two from injury at birth; and when I had the last, the doctor told me he did not know how I had kept one, the times that I had had, and the way they had to use the baby before birth. And now I am suffering myself, all from not being able to take care of myself during pregnancy. My baby that I lost died from haemorrhage when he was eight days old; then the second, when she was four months old, died from an injury to the spine, both done at birth. I think it would have been a good thing for me if all these reforms had been in force, as I should have both been better in health and saved a lot of suffering to myself and my children.

It was from no fault of my husband that I had to suffer: it was from shortness of work. I know I should have had the best of everything if he had been able to get it for me. He had 28s. a week and all holidays off. Then there was out of work, many a time playing for six weeks at a time.

Wages 28s.; six children, one miscarriage.

84. 'Two children under the year.'

I have had seven children, and three have died. I certainly have had very hard, long labours, but I don't know that it could have been avoided; the doctor always said it was in my favour – I am not very strong. But I think what I suffered during my pregnancy most women have to suffer. Although my husband and myself were very ignorant on such matters when we were married, or some of it might have been avoided. That is why I am so pleased it is being made a public question, so that the people will be more enlightened on the subject.

You will see I had my first two children under the year,

all due to ignorance. It nearly sent me in a decline. My husband and myself were very young, and no one had ever talked to me. I am pleased it is different nowadays. I had a daughter married a year last Christmas; her husband and her is as pure yet as the day they married. She is twenty-seven, and her husband thirty years old. They are as happy as two children. They are both well read, and understand things better than I did when I married. They are passionately fond of children, and will go in for one presently.

It is my three last babies I have buried. The doctor says I must not have any more; it will be fatal to me if I do.

Wages 22s. to 26s.; seven children.

85. Effects of worry.

Having suffered with rheumatic fever at the age of five, through going to live in a new damp house, perhaps explains the reason I suffered more than most women during pregnancy and confinement, as I was left with a weak heart all my life. I may also say I have had the same fever three times altogether. I married most happily, and my first miscarriage occurred when I had been married two years, through lack of strength, as I was anaemic. Two years afterwards my little girl was born, strong and healthy, although for nine months I was unable to walk or do my housework, and she has thrived up to the present age of six years. I never recovered my usual health, as I could not afford to rest after my confinement, as I had to work to help pay the debt incurred through my long illness. After one year I was again pregnant, and as I had overworked myself I was again too weak to carry; and thus occurred the second miscarriage, due entirely to having no rest. I suffered two months with haemorrhage that threatened to end my life, but I revived and continued in a weakly state for three years, being just able to do my housework, when my little son was born, strong and healthy, weighing at birth 12 pounds, and has remained healthy up to two years, the present time; and I have fed both children by breast up to two years each, without the aid of stout or intoxicants, milk being my chief diet. Thus you will see that I have had two miscarriages and two lovely babies. If you can understand this jumble of events, you will notice that while I was worried by circumstances I could not bear children, while during both times when I was obliged to rest I was successful, showing that homes of rest for women in pregnancy and confinement would result in a great saving of life, and also result in children being healthy born. Also, the grant advocated would relieve the mother of the necessity to overwork herself.

In reference to my husband's earnings, during the time they varied from 16s. 6d. to 25s. per week. But of course I never received more than the small amount in the winter, and the largest amount in the summer, for housekeeping, as my husband had to lose short time in winter.

Wages 16s. 6d. to 25s.; two children, two miscarriages.

86. 'Not much strength left.'

I am afraid I cannot tell you very much, because I worked too hard to think about how we lived. When my second baby came, I did not know how I was going to keep it. When the last one came, I had to do my own washing and baking before the week-end. Before three weeks I had to go out working, washing, and cleaning, and so lost my milk and began with the bottle. Twice I worked to within two or three days of my confinement. I was a particularly strong woman when I married. There is not much strength left. But, thanks be to God, I have not lost one. I have two girls and three boys, every one strong and healthy.

The firm my husband worked for failed; then for the most times he did not work; but I can truly say that for the most part of twenty-five years 17s. per week was the most I received from him.

Wife's allowance 17s.; five children.

87. Struggles of a miner's wife.

I dare say I could write a book on my early struggles with my seven children, and a miner's home to contend with;

and many a week my husband has not had a penny of wage to bring home, besides the experience of three big strikes and many small ones.

I may say we were married nineteen years before we lost one, and then I lost my baby first, a grand little girl of two. Then, a year and a half after, I lost a fine lad of fourteen in the fever hospital, of scarlet fever and diphtheria. Two years after that we lost a girl of twelve from tubercular disease of the kidneys from cow's milk. The doctor was treating her for eight years for Bright's disease of the kidneys. I brought them up breast-fed, so she must have contracted it after she was weaned. Such a clever child she was. So you will see we have had our troubles.

I may say I had very good times at confinements, except the first and the last. The youngest was born feet first, which was an awful experience, and her heart was nearly stopped beating; so I think that left her heart weak, and she cut her teeth with bronchitis. I used to get up always by the ninth day until the last. I was between forty-one and forty-two when she was born, so had to rest a bit longer, but had to see to household duties as soon as possible.

I am firmly of opinion that if the State wants strong, healthy, useful citizens, they should provide the mothers in the homes with sufficient wages where the husband's wage is inadequate. Nor should married women be allowed to work outside the homes for some stated period before and after childbirth. The men should demand a decent living wage to provide for them at home.

Seven children, one miscarriage.

88. 'Did not like to say anything.'

I can safely say that had there been a centre to which I could have gone before my first boy was born I should have been saved the terrible torture I suffered both before and after confinement. I was very ignorant before marriage, and went away among strangers; and when I became pregnant I did not like to say anything to a strange doctor, and I had no lady friends whom I felt I could confide in. So I went about with an ulcerated stomach, sick after every attempt to take food; and when my baby came, I nearly lost my life. He was also very delicate for five years after birth, wholly due, I am convinced, to the state I was in whilst pregnant.

With the other two boys, I have always had to get about too soon. The month I have always had to have a woman in the house, during which time I have been absolutely helpless, being a terrific expense.

The doctor has ordered me to lie down for two hours each day, but that is absolutely impossible for a working man's wife when she has two or three children around her, meals to provide, and the washing and cleaning, etc., to do in the home.

I speak from my own experience, and I know that there

are thousands of women who are a million times worse off than I am, for I have the best husband in the world; but his nor any other working man's wages won't pay for help in the home at a cost of at least 12s. a week and food. On the very day my first baby was born my husband was thrown out of work. This was kept from my knowledge for five weeks, and I am sure you will guess all the scheming he used to keep me in ignorance. He had his club money for the period he was out of employment, which amounted to 9s. a week.

Wages 25s. to 30s.; three children.

89. A brutal husband.

I have just heard of the following case: A poor woman, only twenty-eight years of age, was confined last Wednesday with her seventh child, all living. She has been allowed to live until this affair is over in a deplorable cottage that is condemned. She has been living quite near for about four months, but I and my neighbours have never seen her nor the two youngest children, aged two and a half years and fifteen months, and we are now told they have no clothes to come out in. These two children were born in the workhouse infirmary. We hear that the father, a hay-carter, only did six weeks' work in a twelvemonth. He must be a most brutal man. He was fighting the poor wife only a fortnight ago, as if she were another man. The poor thing lies there with only an old sheet and quilt for covering, and a poor woman who is attending to the other children has taken the blanket from her own baby to lend her. The very night the baby was born the midwife had to send for a policeman, the husband was carrying on in such a dreadful manner, and was worse afterwards, because they would not let him have the Insurance paper that had just been filled in by the midwife for the Insurance.

90. 'I overdid myself.'

Judging from my own experience, a fair amount of knowledge at the commencement of pregnancy would do a lot of good. One may have a good mother who would be willing to give needed information, but to people like myself your mother is the last person you would talk to about yourself or your state. Although mother nursed me with my first child, I never said one word to her about it coming, except the bare date I expected. I felt I couldn't, and outside people only tell you what garments you need, and just the barest information. I have learned the most useful things since my children have grown up. The youngest is nine. The idea that you impress the child all through the time with your own habits and ways, or that its health is to a great extent hindered or helped by your own well-being, was quite unknown to me.

At the time I fell with my second child we were in very

bad circumstances, and feeding my first with a bottle, I stinted myself all I could to give him plenty; and having moved from one house to another two months before the second one was born, I overdid myself, with the result that I was bad for a week before he was born; and then, the birth being such a long time about, a clot of blood got down into my ankle, and before I got far over the confinement I was laid up with a bad leg, which the doctor said was due to the child being so long coming into the world. I should say I had a midwife this time, as I could not afford the doctor's fee. Had the midwife called in the doctor, as she should have done, I might have been saved a lot, for my back has never been right since. Whenever I get very tired or not very well, I always feel it in the place where he seemed fixed. So I feel that if young mothers knew more of the need for care of themselves, and what should be done for them at the time of childbirth, much suffering could be saved.

Wages 18s. to 32s.; three children, one miscarriage.

91. 'Better to have a small family.'

I have only had the three children, and have been married thirty-two years. In the first place, I was only twenty years old when I had my first baby, and must confess that I suffered a great deal through ignorance, but am pleased to say that I always had all that was really necessary, as regards doctors and nursing. I may say that my husband and myself were quite agreed on the point of restricting our family to our means. If we had not done so, I could not possibly have reared my eldest girl. I was able to have good medical advice and give her plenty of attention day and night.

I may say that I have disgusted some of our Guild members by advocating restrictions. I think that it is better to have a small family and give them good food and everything hygienic than to let them take 'pot-luck.'

Wages £2 to £3; three children.

92. Ignorance.

I feel very keenly myself on the ignorance of young girls getting married and having babies, because I am quite sure some of my sufferings and the death of my babies need not have been.

When my first baby was brought into the world, within a few days of my twenty-first birthday, after three days' labour and agony, the baby was nearly dead. I can hear now the slaps from that doctor on the child to bring life into him, and my own cry of 'Let it die; do not beat it so.' He lived, a lovely boy but a cripple, for nine and a half months, admitted by the doctor to be through the long hours of labour.

A strong point has always been mine that doctors do not give sufficient advice to young mothers. I had to go through the same suffering with my second child, born an epileptic, living three months. My next three girls are alive today, spared, I honestly believe, through my own experience, and the fact of having more humane doctors with instruments. My last baby was literally torn from me. The doctor told my husband he could not save both. They dare not chloroform me, and so I had to bear it. The doctor said I must never have another child. I never have, but why should I have suffered? My first doctor could have said that I was not fitted. I had a good husband, a fairly good income, but when I think of poor women with probably indifferent or bad husbands, how do they live? If our scheme could be brought forward, what a help to know that a woman after a bad time could have a longer rest! Oh, the feeling of knowing that the nurse has gone, and you must wash and dress your own baby! Whereas if the mother could be helped – and the money could do this – how nice she would feel, as she could rest with her little one, after having made it comfortable, by having some help with the housework!

We want all our mothers to teach their daughters, not to keep everything from them, as it was kept from me. If we can only get expecting mothers to attend maternity homes – to see they get a good nurse, not a tippler: they should be banished from the profession ... I thank God that a band of good women are working on the maternity scheme for women.

Wages 32s.; five children.

93. Out-of-door exercise every day.

I had a very natural confinement with both, and a short, sharp time of labour with the first, rather more lingering with the second. My first was what they call a dry labour, and a very sick one – the worst the doctor had had – and it was very exhausting to me. The best times are bad enough, but I was told by the nurse that mine were good times. With the first she stayed a month, and the second three weeks, being called to another case. I think I was very fortunate in having a good mother, who always taught us from childhood how to live to be healthy, and both my sister and I had natural confinements through following her advice when young; that is what makes me so keen on 'Moral Hygiene.' Young women do not take care or have proper exercise enough. Ordinary work does not do the harm. I did all my housework and the washing right up to the time of confinement both times, but I did not white-wash or do papering, as I know some do, and then wonder why they miscarry. Another one I know of insisted on the doctor giving chloroform, as she was sure she would never get through it without. Of course, I am very active, while some are indolent, and that has a great deal to do with it; and I made a practice of getting outdoor exercise every day, if not too far towards the end of the time, and at great inconvenience, as with the boy I had piles very bad, and often had to stop a moment or two before I could go on, but of course it was at night when I went out. I also had heartburn with both a short time, and a bad attack of indigestion, which I never suffer from at other times, but which the doctor soon relieved.

Two children.

94. 'Given anything to have a good sleep.'

There is a great deal of unnecessary suffering entailed on the woman during pregnancy by lack of not knowing what to do, or how to do it, such as having all her own washing and work to do, especially in the latter stages. When a man is only bringing home about £1 a week, and has two or three children, it is impossible for the mother to get proper help or even food. I think it would be a very good thing if something could be done to lighten that burden. I am not speaking as one that does not know. I have had it to do myself, in my early married life, but, thank God, my lot is changed now. I have had eleven children, two still-born, and one miscarriage, so have gone through it. I also think we should try and do something for the mothers after childbed, as many have to be about so soon after, and no doubt that tends to weakening the mother, so that she cannot give her child proper support, and cannot recover her own strength. I do not think any woman ought to attempt anything like hard work until she has had at least a month's good nursing and support after confinement, but it is impossible to do it on a man's pay at £1 or 25s. per week. I have always felt if I could only have another week or so of rest I should feel a different woman, and I am sure most of my poor sisters feel the same. I also think that if children were naturally fed it would be all the better for them. When I was pregnant I would have given anything to have had a good sleep during the day. I used to think it was idleness, and try to shake it off, but I do not think so now, and would give every poor woman all the rest she really needed.

Wages about £1; nine children, two still-born,
one miscarriage.

95. 'Husband who was nurse and mother.'

I was brought up in the country with a cat and a dog for playmates, so when I went among other young people, I was very shy, and never made girl friends. That may account for my ignorance in the things that mattered at the time of my marriage, at the age of twenty-one and a half. My husband was just as ignorant, and we had to pay very dearly for our ignorance. I was married about eight weeks when I became ill; I went to the doctor and took a lot of physic, but was no better, then I would not have any more from the doctor, and tried to doctor myself, but I was very ill the whole of the seven and a half months that I was pregnant. The birth was a forced one. I was taken very ill, and knowing baby should not come for six weeks longer, I was bearing the pain as well as I could, just cheering myself that it would be less to go through when the time came, when my husband came in and would insist on getting a doctor. We tried a new one this time, who lived quite near. He had just left the infirmary, and we had heard he was very clever in maternity. When he saw me and questioned me, he sent for the nurse. The rest of that night is too terrible to go through even now after twenty-eight years. Suffice it to say that next morning there was a poor little baby boy with a very large swollen head dreadfully cut, and a young mother dreadfully cut also. One would have thought the trouble was over now – anyhow, we thought so, but we found it had only begun. A week or two after the pains began. I thought it was all right, that I had not got quite well. At last I had to go to the doctor again. He told me I was going on all right. At the end of six weeks the nurse called. I told her just how I felt, and that the doctor said it was through the bad confinement I had gone through. She told me to tell him to come and examine me thoroughly, that there was something growing there. He came, and when my husband saw him afterwards, he said, 'Oh, there is really nothing. There is a little hardness there, that is all. Your wife is very nervous.' My husband told him that I was anything except nervous. However, I went on for eighteen months, never knowing what moment those terrible pains were going to take me. Many

times it was in the street. I was in bed about eight months
out of the eighteen. Then came a very terrible time, and
my husband called another doctor in, and I was ordered
into the B. Infirmary at once. I got better. I was home three
months, when I was carried in again. They said it was ovar-
ian trouble. They wanted to operate. My husband asked
them how long I might live as I was. They said I might live
for years, but I would always be subject to these attacks. He
told them he would rather keep me as I was than risk an
operation. On inquiring the cause of the trouble, I was told
by the nurse it was confinement. I went on in much the
same way until my boy was ten years old. Then I had to be
operated on. It was a case of life or death then. But if I
went into the Infirmary I could not choose my doctor, so
Dr —— offered to do the operation free, but I would have
to go into a private hospital, which meant a good deal to
us, who hardly knew which way to turn for an extra
shilling then. However, my husband insisted that Dr ——
was to do the operation, and by letting everything else go
he managed to get the money together by the time I came
out, which was three weeks at £3 3s. per week and £1 7s.
6d. for the second nurse. The trouble was a multiple
tumour; it had grown round about the intestines. They had
to tear the one from the other. After leaving the hospital
I was in bed for three months, but it was a complete cure,
though no one except my husband expected me to get
over it. Dr —— told me I could not have gone through a

more serious operation unless I had had my head taken off, and then there was no hope at all.

Now I maintain that if we had understood things relating to married life, all this could have been saved. I would not have starved myself and child before birth for one thing, and I would have been more careful on washing days not to lift tubs or jump to reach lines, neither would I have cleaned windows and a hundred and one other things that a pregnant woman should not do, and, above all, we would not have had an inexperienced doctor.

I must just tell you that my husband has always been husband, nurse, and mother. The pain was never quite so bad when he was near, and no one ever made my bed like him.

Our income, until baby was six months old, was £1 6s. per week. Then my husband got out of employment – was out four months. He took up an agency, and did a very little with it, but with that little and about £2 12s. 6d. we had managed to save, and pawning, we got through without going into debt until he got another job. This lasted about eighteen months, averaging about 30s. per week. Then for about twenty months he averaged about 10s. per week. Our home went then a thing at a time, but we got through at the expense of our insides and outsides, without help or debt, except doctor's bills. Then we came to this town on £1 7s.; after a few years £1 9s. The rise came just two years before I underwent the operation. We had our home to get out of that, and had to get it on the hire system (or borrow from friends, and we both objected to borrowing). Some people say drink is the cause of poverty, but I think you will agree with me when I say we had not enough to drink. Our rent would work out at about 6s. per week. I think this is what you want. Of course, things are very much better with us now, and have been for the last twelve years, both in health and finance. I just want to add that although the first half of my married life was so hard and painful, I would not have missed one bit of it, because it has all helped to make me understand things that matter from a practical point of view. If there is anything more I can help in I shall be pleased to do so.

Wages 26s. to 30s.; one child.

96. Injury at confinement.

I rather shrink from talking about myself on the subject, but if my remarks would help any young mother, I don't so much mind. My husband's average wage was about 24s. a week . . . I helped in the work, as his earnings were not nearly enough as the children came. I had four children at intervals of about two years, whom I was able to nurse, but although I had no illness during pregnancy, with my fifth baby I had a very long illness through the doctor hurrying the birth, instead of giving nature a chance, and he was rough in handling me. Now, the result was a three months' illness, and my baby had to be brought up by bottle.

What was still more serious, I was so injured that for nearly ten years I was an invalid. During that period I had two premature confinements, and several slight miscarriages. Then I got a little stronger, and finally my sixth baby was born without the help of a doctor, because I was so afraid of a repetition of what I had suffered. I am glad to say I gradually recovered, although all my friends thought I would never get well.

I think every expectant mother should have a duly qualified nurse to attend her. I had several miscarriages. There is a better chance now than when I was having my family. Good nursing is necessary. I rejoice to know that the Guild is pressing forward on this matter.

Wages about 24s.; six children, one still-born,
several miscarriages.

97. Childless.

I have had four children, and all were born one year and a half after each other. My two eldest died in one week from whooping-cough, age five and three. Two of my children were still-born. I was very young at the time, and only wish this Maternity Scheme had come out years ago. I have a good husband, but we are childless, I am sorry to say. I am on many committees, and take a great interest where children are concerned.

Wages 18s. to 27s.; two children, two still-births,
one miscarriage.

98. 'I simply struggled on.'

I have had two children. I never was so well in my life as I was during pregnancy over my first. A bearing-down caused haemorrhoids. However, I was not troubled greatly with them then. My second child was born one year and seven months afterwards. Now all the time during pregnancy over him I was thoroughly ill. My work was a trouble, and altogether I *was* ill. But as pregnancy is never thought a sufficient cause for even having a holiday, I simply struggled on for fear of being held up to ridicule. You see, I was only twenty-two years old then, and thought that the only way to do was to show a brave front, even though I felt almost too ill to do anything. Well, I had to have chloroform, and again I had to have instruments; and my children would never be born naturally, for my womb is in the wrong place, the doctor says. I had also a trained nurse who despaired again of my life.

I was in bed one month for maternity and was unable to do my work even when I did get up. I could not mother either of my children, for I never had any milk. That was a grief to me. I had haemorrhoids again through bearing down, brought on through pregnancy, and from these I suffered for three years and doctored for them. Then I had an operation and had them removed. I have not had more children, neither do I want them, as the doctor fears my life will pay the forfeit. I had a serious operation for tumour in the womb four years ago, and have been much better in health ever since.

Two children.

99. Story of a confinement.

My first child was born ten months after my marriage. My husband's age at marriage was twenty-eight years, and my own age twenty-five years, and we are both Londoners, residing all our life in the city of London, until my first-born attained the age of eleven months.

My children have been born quite healthy, and the doctors have said fine babies. But I am pleased to say I am a mother who has had no terrible sufferings to relate as to the sufferings of a long period of labour. Two hours and a half has been the time from the very first stage of labour, until the appearance into this world of each of my children. And I would say, personally, women were never created to suffer as many a one does. I made this remark to my first nurse, and she said, 'You are right.' I had been told such experiences by women who had had families. It is nature, and nature does or should do its own work, she said. Take, for instance, the apple. When it is fully ripe, it falls from the tree. So the child, when the time has arrived for its appearance, I say it should come as naturally, not to look upon the little creature distorted and bruised through having to be brought into the world.

My strong conviction is, as soon as a woman feels the slightest pain she should have immediate attention. You are strong at the commencement, and able to give the help in bringing your baby, but if allowed to go on for hours your strength is exhausted, you have lost that power and vitality which you require, that after hours of suffering artificial means have to be resorted to.

My second child was born at N——. The doctor did his own work and the nurse's too, arriving and leaving the house in half an hour, my mother just taking the baby until the nurse had time to get in the room.

Now, by my third child I will try to show where I think much is at fault by not having immediate attention. My little daughter was born in D——. My husband had at four o'clock to fetch the doctor and nurse (a qualified midwife) nearly two miles away; no other reliable nearer.

They resided a stone's-throw from each other. But on bringing the nurse and explaining while she dressed she was to call the doctor, she would not hear of it, and fairly repudiated the idea of such a quick confinement, sarcastically saying, never in her experience. Well, the doctor was not informed. Previously on engaging them I made it quite

clear how my boys had been born – so quickly. In D——,
I may say in passing, indiarubber gloves are worn by the
nurse on receiving the child, and like all rubber things in
these cases have to be boiled before using. Nurse arrived.
Every single thing was ready for her. There was a bright
fire, and every possible article to lay her hands on, baby's
clothes on the horse airing and warming.

She looked at me in my agony, and said: 'Oh, not likely
to come off yet, ma' (to my mother), and sent the old soul
out for a saucepan to boil the new gloves in. Well, it went
on for a time, until I felt my pains were leaving me, and I
would not trouble any longer; I was tired. But I thought,
no. Why should I suffer? I called to my husband, and he
came to the bedroom door, and I said: 'Fetch the doctor, I
want attention.' He went. The nurse said: 'Well, I know
you have the whole day to go by the look of things. Doctor
will be very cross. He is very busy, and does not like being
brought out of bed. He knows everything is right when I
am on the case.' I felt another little pain, and I made
another effort, my breath almost gone. I called to her, boil-
ing her gloves: 'If you do not leave those blessed things, the
child will be here.' She flew to me, laughing at an unnecessary fuss, but my child was entering the world, two
minutes after my husband had left the house, but, being
certified, she did the doctor's work. But she could not get
the afterbirth, and pushed and fairly punched my stomach
most unmercifully to get it, and I said: 'Well, nurse, I really

cannot stand this any longer. My two previous doctors had said, never be in a hurry for this. Let nature have its course; it will come in time. The doctor will be here soon, and he will soon get it.' The doctor had heard and come in, and told the nurse to see to the baby, who was bitterly cold, and he would see to me. In a very few minutes I was quite comfortable.

The doctor was very cross at not having been notified by the nurse that she was on her way to me, knowing the statement I had given when engaging them.

If there is truth in it or not, I was told later that if all was over and done with before the arrival of the doctor, the nurse was given something out of the fee.

I might say, having my mother with me, I only required the nurse night and morning, and this nurse only went out like that, because she had so many cases she preferred them so. But it happened I did not see her one evening during the time, and on the third day she did not put in an appearance at all, and on the Sunday, two o'clock; other days the times ranged from twelve till three o'clock when she came.

My confinements have been splendid ones, but for all that I feel it is almost, if not quite, three months before a mother feels her strength the same as before. What women feel like who have to turn out shortly after to work hard, I would not like to imagine.

I personally have always felt, besides not having the

usual amount of strength, I have been very forgetful; for instance, I would go to the cupboard and quite forget what I had gone for, and have to stand and think for a little time, and then very likely not know. During pregnancy, my health was always very good, and I was able to do all household duties and washing right up to the time of my confinement. But towards evening I would be tired all over, and be thankful to go to bed. But I usually took a glass of hot milk at bedtime. I found it not only soothed the nerves, but induced sleep. I took a dose of castor oil once a fortnight.

I have nursed all my children for ten months, not allowing a particle of any kind to pass their lips in the way of foods but my own milk until nine months old, and then gradually weaned them off.

I have stated above feelings to show what a woman feels who does not endure great sufferings in childbirth.

My strong conviction is that unless there is anything wrong internally, and a woman takes a bit of care as to what she eats and drinks during pregnancy, and has, as I say, immediate attention, much suffering would be alleviated.

I am the average working man's wife, who spends most of her time looking to the needs of an old mother, husband, children, and home, cutting and contriving to make the weekly income go as far as one possibly can, attending the Guild as quite a change, and seeking to obtain as much knowledge of the Women's Movement on to Progress; and where, here and there, I may be able to pass an opinion, I do; and try to live, that when I have passed away the world will be none the worse for my being in it.

Wages £1 15s. to £2 5s.; three children.

100. A wreck at thirty.

I had seven children and one miscarriage in ten years and three months. This left me at the age of thirty a complete wreck. My great difficulty was during pregnancy, suffering very severely from sickness, so much so, indeed, that on two occasions I was under the doctor the whole of the time. The doctor gave me his services free.

I tremble even now to think what my life would have been but for his kindness to me. I could not have paid for a doctor, as wages were only £36 a year, and I had to pay £10 a year rent out of that. When I look back upon those days I wonder how we did live.

My last child was born a delicate, weak child, who suffered from malnutrition until she was eleven months old, and at her birth the doctor told me I should never have another strong and healthy baby, and that women should only have a child every three years, and rest at least a month after confinement. He knew I could not give myself the rest I needed, for I could not afford to pay anyone to look after my home and children. I had to rely upon some child of thirteen who was able to leave school, and whose parents were glad of the 2s. 6d. a week I could ill afford to pay. I have been forced on many occasions to do things no woman lying-in should have done. I have left my bed on the tenth day, and have had to do the family washing as early as a fortnight.

I do feel most strongly that women should be able to get advice and help during pregnancy. Our children are a valuable asset to the nation, and the health of the woman who is doing her duty in rearing the future race should have a claim upon the national purse. Ample provision should be made so that she could give of her best.

Wages 10s. to 14s. and husband's food; seven children and one miscarriage.

101. Two children in eighteen months.

I have only had two children. I was married at the age of twenty-three. My husband was twenty-five. I had been married just eleven months when my first baby was born. Now, as soon as ever I knew I was pregnant, I set about (with the help of a considerate and helpful husband) taking the greatest care of myself for the sake of the babe unborn, in such things as diet, exercise, fresh air, etc. I did no very heavy work. My husband and I did the washing in the evening, he did all the dollying and wringing, and helped me in many ways. The result was I had a fine and healthy baby, and during pregnancy I was so well myself, and I had everything a working man's wife could have to make things as easy as possible. I had no worry of any kind, and that I consider a great comfort to a woman.

At my confinement I had a doctor and a nurse, and if I had not had what I believe is called a dry labour, I should have had the easiest of times (and they are bad enough), but the water broke at 6 a.m., and my baby was not born till 4.30 p.m.

My baby was never the slightest trouble. I had been in the nursery before I was married, both as nurse and nursery governess, so my baby had all the care and attention I had been taught to bestow on babies. I was sorry to find, when my baby was a year old, that I was again pregnant. I had breast-fed my baby up till then, for she had cut no teeth till she was eleven months old, although she was strong and well and running about at nine months old; of course, I weaned her at once. We were very disappointed to find I was going to have another baby so soon after the first. We had not intended this to happen. However, I made the best of it, and had a son when the daughter was eighteen months old. I was not so well carrying the second baby, and he was as great a handful when a baby as my first baby was no trouble, and by the time he was six months old I was very weak and ill. I think having the two children so quickly, and nursing my first baby so long, had been a great strain. The second child was not so strong a baby as the first. He suffered from teething eczema, and I lost a great deal of rest. My second confinement was fairly good, although I had thought the baby was coming two or three times before he came, labour pains came on and went away; and when my boy was born the doctor said if he had been another half-hour in the birth, he would have been dead. I should have sent for a doctor a week previously, but not knowing the exact time to expect my baby, I did not want to send for the doctor until it was really necessary.

I never had any more children. I was ill and weak for a long time while having to nurse my second baby, and having them so quickly. How women, and poor women, can have children year after year, is a marvel to me. I know of cases here close to where I live, where a consumptive mother is having babies nearly every year. To me it seems terrible, bringing such children into the world, a burden to their parents, to themselves, and to the nation, for they are only wrecks, and fill our hospitals, mental deficiency schools, and prisons. But the cases are so common. Where they are poorest, where they have not enough to live on and keep their present family decently, they still have more children.

I am sure there is great need for thought and care being given to the mother previous to childbirth and afterwards, and I do feel that a scheme as is suggested is a good one, and that the public health authority should deal with all maternity cases. It would mean untold happiness to the coming generations. It will be grand to get a maternity benefit such as you suggest, and it is most necessary. We have some women in the Guild who feel we should be more independent than take such sums as maternity benefit. They do not realise that we pay rates and taxes just as property owners do, though indirectly.

How some of our poorest women exist year after year, bearing all, I cannot understand. For, if having two children, as I did, in eighteen months wrecked my health, which it did for a long time – and only through having one of the best of husbands was I helped to pull through – I wonder what so many other less fortunate women suffer. It is just slavery and drudgery.

Wages 28s.; two children.

102. Need for nourishment after confinement.

For what I can see of others, I came off fairly well; but, in the first instance, my first child was a girl. I was very well during pregnancy, but being such a strong child the doctor told me to give it the bottle; but, on the other hand, the nurse persuaded me to keep it to the breast. The result was as soon as I got about, by keeping the child to the breast, I had two gathered breasts. I had the two breasts in slings till they broke. The next two being boys – two years between – I was right well during pregnancy. But as soon as a mother is able to get up and have to work, that is the time her health fails her, for she finds she has to feed the rest of her little family, and goes without her own food, and then, through lack of nourishment, often mothers have to go to their bed again.

In the first place, when we were married my husband was a fireman. We ran along smoothly, and up to the time my first and second child was born his standing wage was 30s. a week and overtime. The time went on, and in two years the second was born. Now, just before it came it was my husband's turn to go to pass for engine driver. The result was he failed to pass the eyesight test. It was a great shock to us both, more so to my husband. It was then the dots they had to count at a distance. They then reduced him to 21s. a week to work in the shed, so we thought it was cruel to run the risk of more family on such a wage. To keep my home up and keep the children respectable I had to take in two young men lodgers, which we have done till I started the children to business. Of course, I take it you don't want to know the ups and downs of life between these times. I must say I have had the best of husbands, or else I should not have been alive now.

If there could be such a thing as a Maternity Club started it would be a benefit to all married women, because the majority of us have to screw and save for confinement, where we ought to be able to have good food and more nourishing food while we are carrying the child, but often have to go with less.

Wages 21s. to 30s.; three children, one miscarriage.

103. Her 'lot.'

Your letter to hand reminding me of my promise to let you have a few details of my neighbour's life. At first she hesitated about telling anything, as she said it was all past and done with, and at times felt ashamed at having had thirteen children, especially to a man like her husband (who is a drunkard). She looks back on her past life at the age of forty-eight with different feelings to what she had at thirty. Then she thought it was her 'lot,' as she terms it, to have so many children, and so many sickly ones, but now she feels she has been to blame for many things – for instance, for the number of children she has had; for the dullness and lack of energy in two of them; for the feeble-mindedness in a third; deafness and sore eyes in a fourth. She blames the conditions under which she bore those children during pregnancy. She was married at nineteen, and a mother before she was twenty, with no knowledge whatever of the duties of motherhood. Her first five children came in rapid succession. While she was pregnant of her sixth child her husband fell out of work, and was out of work six months. During this time they had 10s. a week to live on (from the husband's trade union). She went out washing and cleaning up to the last week of her confinement. While cleaning windows at one of the houses she slipped and fell, hurting her side. Three days later the child was born, apparently all right, but as time went on the mother noticed there was something wrong, but nobody seemed to know what. This child did not cut its teeth till two years old, nor walk without help till it was seven, and now, at the age of eighteen, you can hardly make out a word he says. He is not exactly an imbecile, but he is feeble-minded, and all this could have been avoided could the mother have had proper nourishment during pregnancy, and less work. The mother had to work hard all day, and got little rest at night, as the fifth child was weakly and ailing, and the neighbour who looked after the child during the day used to put gin in its milk to stop its crying, which it did till the effects of the gin had passed off. The poor mother, not knowing that gin was given to the child, would often, after a hard day's work, spend most of the night pacing the bedroom floor, trying to soothe the fretful child, and often had to go downstairs because the crying disturbed her husband. It was not until her sixth child came, the feeble-minded one, that the neighbour admitted giving it gin. Consequently the lad has grown up dull, never made any headway at school. He is a labourer, and twenty years of age, and will never be anything else but a labourer, because, as his mother says, he has no 'head-piece,' and cannot do a simple sum in arithmetic to save his life. The mother firmly believes her children would have been as bright as anybody's could she have had proper nourishment during pregnancy, and herself cared for them after they were born. Her girl of sixteen is deaf in one ear, and has weak eyes, the after-effects of measles when a child. The mother nursed this child a fortnight, then was obliged to leave her with a neighbour while she went out to work. The neighbour neglected the child in letting her run out too soon, etc., and as there were no school clinics when her children went to school, some of them are suffering today from diseases which might have been cured, could they have had attention at the proper time. Now that they are grown up they seem fairly healthy, though undersized, but when one considers their childhood, the want of sufficient food, lack of fresh air (the younger ones always slept four in bed, two at the top and two at the bottom), one wonders they are as healthy as they appear to be. They seem to be fairly good workers, but not one good scholar among them. And to add to the above discomforts, they had a drunken, brutal father. He was never a real father, a surly, gloomy man, never a kind word for his children, and not one of them remembers a caress from him. I can quite understand the woman being ashamed of bearing thirteen children to a man like him, and having to rear them in surroundings and conditions which she has reared hers. It takes it out of the mother mentally and physically.

Wages 16s. to 30s.; thirteen children.

104. Need of rest.

I am perfectly well aware of the urgent necessity of both mother and child receiving proper nourishment and attention. With regard to myself, the one great drawback to me was the fact that I was not able to suckle any of my children, owing to my breasts not being properly developed, so that the child could not draw the nipple. In consequence of this my children had to be fed by the bottle, although I am pleased to say they have thriven and are quite healthy children. Also, prior to confinement, I suffered very much with varicose veins, and felt the need of not being able to have rest, as I had got to be about my work. Also, after confinement, I have been about again in a fortnight, which I should not advise young mothers now to do. I may say that I do think that getting up so soon is the cause of all the misplacements that we hear so much about. However, I am pleased to tell you that I am fortunate in having a considerate husband, which of course is something to be thankful for. My heart aches when I think of women who have brutes to contend with. In my opinion, women should have every kindness shown to them during pregnancy; also means to obtain advice and everything to insure that the unborn child shall have a good start from birth.

Wages 28s. to 40s.; three children.

105. 'Never lost a moment's sleep.'

I am a very busy body, and have not been blessed with a great deal of this world's goods, having had an ailing husband, whom I lost when the youngest was not two years old. But at those times mentioned in your circular I always enjoyed good health. No sickness, as so many women have; of course, days when not feeling quite well. But I do think many women do not give themselves a chance. They seem to give way too much to feelings, and lie about instead of interesting themselves in their work and always keeping hands and minds employed. I had heavy labour times, but did not keep to my bed any longer than I could help, generally feeling able to be up after the fourth day for a little while; then each day a little longer. I often think lying in bed weakens very much, and if able to rise, it is much better to do so, both for baby and self. Of course, not to work as though you had not been through a trying time, and needed to be careful, but at the end of ten days I was always able to do my own work all right, at the same time being able to take good plain food, and making an abundance of milk for the baby. They were such well fed, fat, healthy, happy, contented children, and I never lost a moment's sleep in my life with them. I never used myself to take stout and beer to make milk, as many of the mothers in the North believe in. In the North here, the working class mothers have to work very hard, and they all seem (or in a general way) not to make a trouble of child-bearing. They do not coddle themselves, but just work a not-up-to-the-mark feeling off, which is certainly by far the best way. And about the care of baby, cleanliness is the first care. Then mother's milk if possible, and with perseverance, most mothers could manage to diet themselves to make plenty of milk, but the bottle is the laziest way. Then, of course, baby can be left in another's care, whereas if on the breast, you must take baby with you. I have never had an afterpain after any of them, and soon pulled up again. Once the instruments were used after a weary wait, but I think the women who work have the easiest time. With my last baby I had what made me think of labour pains, every night for a fortnight, and when she came I had only about three pains, and she was born before I could rap for help, and no pain whatever. Do you not think I have been one of the lucky ones? But really many in this condition are like children. They do not want overmuch sympathy or they reckon themselves martyrs straight away, instead of bracing themselves to go through a time of weariness. I have not come across in my experience any who have suffered so acutely, unless in one case, where two of her babies grew to her womb, and had to be brought away by force.

Another woman had a big, broad-shouldered husband, and was herself a very small woman, and it was a case of force every time, and she has had fourteen children, and the same to go through every time, but was able to be up soon, as she soon mended and regained her strength.

Two children.

106. 'I was locked up in a morning.'

I have been a very healthy woman, and pregnancy never upset me very much, but I think if the Maternity Scheme had been in force when I was having children it would have been a great benefit to me. Being very poor, I had to get up on the third day, three or four times, not being able to pay for someone to look after me. My first baby I was locked up in a morning at half-past four, food put so that I could reach it until my husband came home at four in the afternoon, to help myself with everything with regard to the baby. My second was just the same. After that we removed a bit nearer the works, and I did better. We were a very comfortable lot of neighbours, and we always did for one another. I don't say that it was not very hard, because it was, and a little money help would have been a great boon to some of us more than others. With regard to wages, it is rather a sore point. My husband has earned a very good wage nearly all our married life, but he is a born gambler. I never had £1 a week, and a great many times I

i have been a very healthy woman and
pregnancy never upset me very much,
but i think if the Maternity Scheme
had been in force when i was having
children it would have been a great
benefit to me, being very poor i had to get
up on the third day, 3 or 4 times not being
able to pay for someone to look after me.
my first baby i was looked up in a morning
at halfpast 4, food put so that i could
reach it until my husband came home
at 4 in the afternoon, i had no one to help me

had nothing, so that when my children began to work, it took years to pay for what they had to have to be brought up. I have had ten children; nine alive at the present time; six married; three have received the Maternity Benefit and have found it a great help, and feel that it is a credit to everyone who helped to bring so great a scheme about for the benefit of the working man's wife.

Wife's allowance less than £1; ten children, one still-birth.

107. 'Felt like giving in altogether.'

I have had two children. I might say I felt better during pregnancy with the first one than I had ever felt in my life, but I had a very bad time at the birth with instruments, and after three years, when I had the second one, I never felt well, and did not seem to have strength enough to drag through day after day. But I, like a good many more, could not afford to go to the doctor; and with the second baby I had to have instruments again to bring the baby into the world, after which for about eight months I never seemed to regain my strength, and life was a weary existence. Also, I am sorry to say, I had not one of the most careful of husbands, and have always had to make my own provision for the time on £1 a week, and very often nothing, as at that time he would think nothing of staying out all night, and gambling away all his week's earnings. I have always struggled and managed to keep his club paid, so that I had the

30s. from the club to pay the nurse and doctor. For the rest, I have happened to have two good sisters near to me, who always did whatever they could for me, but as to nourishment, I have never been able to get much of that, and have always thought that was what kept me back. I have fortunately been very handy with my needle, and have been able to earn a good bit at times by taking in needlework, or I don't know whatever I should have done. But I am pleased to say, that since I had a breakdown last year, about this time, and was sent away for one month through our Guild Convalescent Fund, my husband has been very much better. I think he had time to find he missed me. Of one thing I am quite sure. I have had as big a struggle as a good many of my womenfolk, but where some have no friends and no talent for earning, I have been more fortunate in being able to do so. I may tell you that when I joined the Guild, nearly five years ago, I had very nearly lost all my spirit, and felt like giving in altogether, but the Guild has done a lot for me in that sense, as I have felt that I must go on doing my duty, and fighting for the right, although sometimes it is very hard. Still, I have always the Guild to look forward to, and have found amongst our members some real good friends, and I shall never forget the great benefit I have felt from the thorough rest and change of the month at the Rest Home. I feel a different woman. Although I am not over-strong, still, I have regained my strength, and a little more energy. I had one miscarriage five years ago, at ten weeks, and my husband was out of work, so I did not have any doctor, but had to keep about and do the best I could, taking just whatever rest I could get. I was months and months getting strong again.

Wages 24s. to 26s.; two children, one miscarriage.

108. Extra well.

As regards myself during pregnancy, I have always been extra well, which I daresay is due to the fact of having been in a position to be able to have all that is required – rest and help in the home, and good nourishing food. Others who are not in the same position have my heartfelt sympathy.

Four children, one miscarriage.

109. Work in a brickyard.

I am very pleased to say that, having one of the best of husbands, I suffered nothing during pregnancy, only ailments of my own caused through my mother having to work in the brickyard during her pregnancy with me. That, I am sorry to say, is the cause of my own and sister's illness – working hard, knocked about, and poorly fed, a good mother, but a rogue of a father; and that thing will go on until women give up hard work during pregnancy.

110. Husband with typhoid fever.

During the first three months of pregnancy with my first baby I suffered fearfully with my head. Then, as time went on, I gradually got better, and able to do my work, and felt quite strong until about the sixth month. Then water began to trouble me; my feet and legs were very much swollen, so much that I could not get any boots on, and had to remain indoors the rest of the time. On the day of the birth I commenced with pains at six o'clock in the morning, and I went on all day, until a quarter to seven at night, and I was getting so weak that the doctor asked me if he might use the instruments. I was glad to have them, but they gave me a fine putting up. The doctor said that my baby could not have been born without them. No doubt it relieved me at the time, but I suffered afterwards, as I was all torn with the instruments, and had to be stitched. I was so weak afterwards that I could not get up on to my elbows, and it took me a considerable time to get my strength up again. At the same time my husband was in bed with an attack of typhoid fever. We had no hospital in our district then. My doctor was very much afraid that I would contract the disease, but I am thankful to say that I escaped. With my second boy I was in good health all the time, and had a quick birth, and without instruments. That was two years and two months after. About four years after the birth of my second boy I had a miscarriage, which I reckon are worse than having a baby, as they nearly drain your system and you suffer severe pain, and it makes you very weak. I always blamed the miscarriage for an attack of nervous debility I had. I first commenced to lose flesh, then my nerves were affected, and I got so weak that I used to faint away several times in the day. My doctor ordered me away for a change, and to get into company, as I was getting so low, but it took me a long time to pick up. About nine years after the birth of my second boy I had a girl, which I am pleased to say put new life into me; it seemed to renew my whole system. She is now eleven years old, and quite strong and healthy.

Wages 27s. 6d. to 42s.; three children, one miscarriage.

111. 'Too exhausted to eat.'

I have been one of the more fortunate women; being fairly strong, my sufferings have not been so heavy as a lot of poor women. At the same time, I was often so poorly that if I had had means to get a little help at times it would have been a blessing. My husband has never earned more than from 23s. to 25s. a week, and many a time I have had to go without many a thing that would have done me good. When I was expecting my last baby, I think it was with going such a long time, and the others, some of them, at work, and coming in to meals. I know I used to get the dinner cooked and struggle through the serving, then I was done, and was obliged to lie down a bit, often without my dinner, as I was too exhausted to eat, and the pleasure of the rest was partly spoiled by the thought of the dinner-table still laid. A bit of help then would have been a boon. But having a good husband smoothed many things over. But this shows that many a woman is unable to do her work, and if the husband is a thoughtless man, or even a bad one, her lot is a hard one indeed. Then, after confinement, women should not be obliged to work, in my opinion, for three weeks, but most working women have to do. I never could possibly keep a woman more than a fortnight – and the struggle during pregnancy of saving up 30s., which was the sum we always aimed for, and it was a big job. Some weeks I have had to be content with putting 3d. away, with the hope of 9d. next week to make it into a shilling. To my mind, this is one of the hardest tasks a working woman has.

Wages 18s. to 25s.; seven children.

112. Thirteen births and four miscarriages.

I am afraid many mothers, like myself, will find it almost impossible to explain our sufferings. During pregnancy we do not all suffer alike, but to me it was nine months of misery. But I had to work all the time. My husband's wages were only £1 a week, and he had to lose all wet weather.

With my fourth child he was out of work twelve weeks in the bitter winter. I worked as dressmaker with a machine nearly night and day, and when the baby was brought into the world with instruments, I nearly lost my life, and could not be moved for nearly a fortnight. My ninth son, I was working at a lady's house when near my confinement, and in putting down a carpet I hurt myself very much, and was very ill until my baby was born, and then he was born a cripple – would have always walked on his ankles, with the soles of his feet together. But I used to take him to the hospital for a long time, and he is able to get his own living now. So you will see it takes all energy and hope and joy out of a woman's life, when they have to work the whole time through no fault of their own or their husbands, but just to keep the home together.

Wages £1; twelve children, one still-birth, four miscarriages.

113. An agricultural labourer's daughter.

I have only had one child, a daughter, who is now six years. I had been married eight years when she was born, but have had no miscarriages. I was very well when I was pregnant. The mothers in the Guild were most kind in advising me during pregnancy, at the time and after. I weaned her at nine months, and she is one of the bonniest girls one can see.

My husband, *when in work*, earns a good wage. It has

been his experience to be out of work many times, for varying lengths of time – once for fourteen weeks – that soon
after our child was born.

In an agricultural district, large families and small wages
predominate. I am the second child of a family of twelve,
and as my father's earnings were very small it always meant
my mother working too – hop-tying, gathering fruit, har-
vesting, and even picking stones off fields. As soon as each
of us was old enough we had to work very hard; at ten and
eleven years of age I worked in the fields, and did shaving
poles, etc. My mother had to pay 9d. and 11d. per week
school money, out of her little, for us, and I am thankful to
her for educating us as she did, never keeping us away to
mind babies, as a great many did in those days. I am nearly
thirty-nine now, and free education had not come in then.

Wages 24s. to 40s.; one child.

114. 'No rest for mothers, night or day.'

I remember it was a very big struggle to get all that was
quite necessary for ourselves and the expected baby.
Although my experience was far before thousands of
others – should I say, women, when I was only just turned
eighteen?

In the first place, I felt a doctor would be too expensive,
so only had a midwife. Things were not just right with
baby, so I had to call in a doctor and pay £1 5s. My nurse

I only engaged for a fortnight, then thought I could manage, but I took cold, and had a most awful gathered breast, and had to go back to bed again for another week or two. When my baby was five months old I began to turn against my food; was nursing baby at the time, so did not think for one moment I could be pregnant again, but it was so. When the second one came, the first was unable to walk, I can assure you. You need not wonder at women doing all they can to prevent having big families, for there is certainly no rest for mothers night or day.

I can tell you I saw but very little pleasure the first part of my married life. I married in 1884. I had two children, lost one, and lost my husband by consumption in June, 1887. He needed the best of everything. It used to cost nearly 5s. per week for one sort of medicine he felt did him good, so you see there was very little to do with. I was only twenty-two when he died. I believe now, when I think about it, my baby could have been spared had I had more experience; although I did my best and was a good mother, as far as lay in my power, but there was no one to advise me. So you can imagine ours was one continual struggle from beginning to end, and then not so bad as many others. When I look back on that time I feel very sad. I believe my husband was in receipt of £1 5s. per week, but I am not quite sure; he was a policeman, so it was regular, and of course not many clothes to buy. Living in a village, our rent was small. This will, I am afraid, be little to assist you, but it is all I can tell you. It would not be possible to tell you all one feels with one baby and the expected one, and all work to do. No one could imagine who has never been through it.

Wages 25s.; two children.

115. Proper care.

With regard to myself, fortunately I have always had the proper care, with the result that I had normal times.

My first child (a boy) died when he was eight months old. My health broke down, and he had to be taken from the breast, no food agreed with him, convulsions set in, and my loved one died. I was three years, then had another (a girl). Two years and nine months after that I had another girl. Both these are now fine young women. The proposed scheme to 'link up the State with the home and the municipality under one authority' is just what is wanted in all towns and cities. Much suffering would be saved and many lives spared.

From the advice that mothers have been able to get at the 'Baby Welcome' here, many babies' lives have been saved. But this is voluntary, and a fortnight ago a week was set apart to go from house to house for subscriptions in every district, as the work could not go on without funds.

Wages 27s. 6d. to 35s.; three children.

116. Eight miscarriages.

I have not had any children to bring up, but I have had the misfortune to have had eight miscarriages, the last one as far back as 1898, when I had to go to the infirmary for an operation, and I have not had any since. But you must understand they have not been brought on by neglect or ill use, but by my having a severe attack of influenza in 1891 before I was married, which left me with weakness of the womb. I had to be attended by the doctor every time.

No child, eight miscarriages.

117. Need for municipal midwives.

I have had two average children – one a boy aged nine years, the other a girl aged four years. As regards pregnancy, I had general good health – though I felt rather faint at times in the first and second month – up to the seventh month, and then I used to feel rather bad some days – cramp in my legs, etc. I have been able to keep my house going up to the time of confinement (my husband being a mechanic, I had to do the housework and washing and cooking). I must tell you I am a teetotaler, and during pregnancy I used every morning to take fine groats with plenty of milk. I still took them every morning and evening after my babies were born, and I had sufficient milk for them until I weaned them, starting from ten months and finishing them altogether at one year. Neither of them had any fits or convulsions, my boy's first illness being at the age of five and half years, and my little girl has not had an illness yet. At the present time they are both well in health. I think I should dearly like to see State maternity nurses, for this way there is the greatest difficulty in securing a nurse. I know from one or two of my friends and from my own experience we were all greatly worried at not being able to secure good nurses. As you are aware, many of them drink, and others don't care to come when there are other children to look after. I had a doctor, and had to pay 14s. a week for a nurse. I think expectant mothers should not be allowed to work in factories, etc., when they are pregnant, for you want as much fresh air as possible. Taking an average year, with all holidays, I think my husband's wages would amount to 35s. weekly. He is in the black line and a Socialist, and we both cannot think how working people, especially Co-operators, can be otherwise.

Wages 35s.; two children, one miscarriage.

118. Easy circumstances.

As you will see on the attached form, I am not able, as a mother, to give my experience of suffering during pregnancy or after childbirth. I was able to have good attention both before and after the birth of my boy, so that any special information other than the ordinary childbirth pains I cannot give.

I suppose my experience will go to prove that proper attention to health, such as you wish expectant mothers to have, would do away with a good deal of the suffering and pain connected with maternity. The opinion of myself and my husband is that none but skilled doctors and nurses should attend at childbirth. I have known many cases in our district where the ordinary midwife has had mothers in pain for hours, only to send for a doctor in the end.

One child.

119. Nothing unusual.

Nothing unnatural or unusual seemed to happen in my case.

Wages 35s. to £2 5s.; three children.

120. Sock-making at twopence a pair.

I will give you the following concerning my married life. First let me tell you I was in the place I was married from just five years as children's maid. I was twenty-five, my husband twenty-six the day we married. Many, including my relatives, thought I ought to have married better. I had been engaged previously, but he turned out to be not the God-fearing man I thought. Then our married gardener asked me to tea, and I met my husband that is now, a true follower of Christ. And I must tell you, the two years we courted we only missed Church twice. I soon saw he had won my heart, but his wages was then poor, but I remembered my dear mother's words – money does not bring happiness; and so we were married against the wishes of my friends, and took two rooms and furnished them. But, oh! I soon found out how hard it was to keep our little home on 24s. a week, 7s. for our two rooms. Then I got a night now and again waiting at table with the lady I had lived with and her friends. How I pleaded to be kept all right, as I could not see our way clear to have a baby in the home, and I would not, could not, let any of our friends know the hard struggle I had. I have a dear, loving husband, who agreed we would like a baby, but had no means of providing for it. I must tell you I had bad health (bloodlessness) before I was married, which cost me a lot of money. Then when we had been married two years I found I was in a certain condition. I hid my condition, and went still waiting at table, until after a big dinner I fainted, and had to own I was so. Then came the shortage of money. I began to stint myself in order to provide for my little one. Many a time I have had bread and dripping for my dinner before my husband came home, and said I had my dinner, as I would not wait. Then I was ill, and had to have the doctor. He said I was run down, and away went some of the little store I had been able to get together. I would not let my friends know how we stood, remembering what they said before I was married. Then came headache after headache, as I worried to know wherever was all the money to come from to provide the funds for doctor and nurse. My sister, who was very proud, and unmarried, engaged me a nurse at 14s. a week for three weeks. She thought she was helping me by seeing that I had a good nurse, but this only added to my worry. Then my husband, thinking to help me get the money, had a knitting machine on the hire system, and made socks and stockings. I had to sew up the toes and press them into shape. I could not get them right for a long time, and this added another worry, as we had to pay each month for the machine, which was a failure. I worked hard at them right up to the time my boy was born. Oh, my poor head, how it ached, as I tried and tried to do them right; and we only got 2d. a pair for making them, and my husband used to walk to the city to the shop with them. (They found the wool.) I had a very bad confinement, and the baby was almost gone when it came into the world. I had no strength to go through. The doctor would not allow me to see anyone for nine days. This was twelve years ago. My boy, although fat, suffers so much with his head. He had a brain and nerve breakdown two years ago, and was ill eleven months. One day the doctor said: 'How were you when you carried this child?' Painful though it was, I told him all. 'Ah,' he said, 'now we know the cause of all this trouble.' I have suffered with my head ever since.

His heart also is slightly affected. If only I could have gone to someone who would have understood, not my relatives, and got some nourishment. All this that he now suffers, I am sure, is the result of my having to work and worry so much while I was carrying. I might say the nurse was very extravagant, and the second week I lay so ill I missed a photo machine my husband had, and learnt – oh, it is almost too painful to write – that he had pawned it for 7s. 6d. to help get me nourishment. He said: 'Never again will you go through this. You are too dear to me.' Well, six years ago, my boy being six years old, my husband had got on, and his wages increased. We had a little girl, which we had always longed for, only to lose it as soon as it came into the world, for I have no strength in my inside (the doctor said) to bring a child into the world. All this weakness, you see, the result of the first confinement. Of course, now, the doctor says it would not be safe for me to have another child. I have a dear loving husband who does all in his power to keep me right. But it is hard to think if I had another it would go or be delicate. Now is there not great need for a place where a young mother could go and get advice and, if necessary, nourishment? I was one who thought I could do a lot on a little a week, and when I found out my mistake would do anything rather than let my friends know their words had come true. I remember when carrying my baby to have to wait for a loaf of bread until my husband came home at five with his money, as I always paid down for all we had. I must tell you we have been married fifteen years and are *very, very* happy.

Wages 24s.; one child, one still-birth.

121. Natural times.

During these times I have been well looked after, and had quite natural times.

Wages 23s. to 45s.; three children.

122. Ironing and kneading in bed.

I was married one year and five months before my first boy was born. I nearly lost my life. I was in labour from 1 o'clock in the morning until 7.5 at night. Then the doctor used instruments. He stated I had worked too hard, and not rested sufficiently, but I could not afford a girl. My husband then was only getting £1 1s. per week, and 5s. rent had to be paid out of it. The second baby came fifteen months after ... I had no milk for either. I was in labour with the second from Monday dinner-time until Tuesday night. Then the doctor gave me an injection of warm water; as I was torn so badly before, he did not want to use the instruments. Two years after I had a miscarriage ... I then had to lie in bed for a whole month. I kept a small girl, and I used to do my own ironing and knead my bread in bed unknown to the doctor. I had a bed put down in the small parlour to save the girl and children running upstairs. I feel sure that if I had had a maternity benefit then to help me, I should not be suffering now inwardly. No mother can stay in bed very comfortably knowing things are going on anyhow while she is in bed. Then, again, during the time she is carrying the child, her mind is troubled, and she becomes fretful, hence a fretful, delicate child. The mother, when funds are low, goes without much food, pleading headache, etc., so as to try and blind her husband. I think an expectant mother should rest at least half an hour every day, and especially towards the last should have no heavy work to do, such as washing and ironing. The extra weight she is carrying naturally throws the humours into her legs, the veins standing out like thick cords, and at night she cannot sleep for cramps and aches. The child is the asset of the nation, and the mother the backbone. Therefore, I think the nation should help to feed and keep that mother, and so help to strengthen the nation by her giving birth to strong boys and girls. She does not require weaklings, and insufficient food and overwork and worry is the root of this weakness, both in the case of mother and child. I only hope that sick visitors should see that it is the mothers that are getting the benefit of the maternity benefit, and not the husband, and often the landlord.

Wages 20s. to 23s.; two children.

123. Tea and sugar put away.

My experience of child-bearing has been very painful, owing to an inward growth. Each confinement was a very critical time – in fact, with the last one I nearly lost my life, and was told by my doctor never to run the risk again. Fortunately for us all, I have a thoughtful husband, or, of course, it would have made the home very unhappy. During the time of pregnancy I used to put a little away every week, perhaps one week tea, another sugar, and so on, as my husband's wages were small, and I could not go out to work, not being strong. I am sure the 30s. the mothers get now would have been a great boon in my case. It would have saved a lot of worry as to ways and means. No one knows what it means to a mother at such times, what contrivances she has to make things eke out. I think myself half the suffering in after-life is brought about by worrying to make ends meet at such times. In my own case, how much I have to be thankful for with a good, steady husband! I honestly think no woman should have less than £1 per week for housekeeping purposes, and how many thousands have far less! I should like to see all workers receiving a living wage, as then I think most of the trouble would be met.

Wages 20s. to 30s.; three children.

124. Six to feed on sixteen shillings.

I have only had four children, but I am pleased to say I have had what we call comfortable times. But I must tell you, since I had my second one, my husband has only earned 16s. a week. I have had a very hard struggle to get through, but, thank the Lord, I have done it. If the Maternity Benefit had been in force, then it would have made it much better. I think the scheme is a beautiful thing, and I think the women should have it. But we have not all got the same kind of husbands. Mine is a very good husband. I was very queer after my last was born, but what could you wonder at – that money to keep six of us? But we are getting over the hardest place, I hope. My eldest is thirteen.

Wages 16s. to 22s.; four children.

125. 'Worked too hard as a girl.'

I have been married seventeen years, and have had four children. My first, a boy, was born two years after marriage. The second was twin boys, born two years and six months after the first. One of these was stillborn. During the whole time of second pregnancy I was very ill and unable either to work or walk about without great pain, the result of trying to do just the necessary housework. At my confine-ment, the afterbirth came first, then the still-birth, and the living child came last. This was very dangerous to me, and I was unable to leave my bed for three weeks, and I was at least three months before I was in my usual health. My third child was born nine years after second (a girl) the after-birth again coming first, the baby being born nine hours after. She lived six hours, and was convulsed from birth. The doctor's opinion was that I had worked too hard as a girl lifting heavy weights, therefore weakening the whole system. It is high time that something was done by the Government to lessen the sufferings of mothers, which has always been hidden as something not to be talked about.

Wages 36s.; three children, one still-birth.

126. A strong woman.

I have not a word to say against any of my child-bearing or pregnancy times, as I have been a strong woman, and have a very good husband. But I always provide for such times. I always had a doctor and midwife, and someone to look after my home, and always stop in bed a long time. I have not had any use for instruments or chloroform. But one thing, I am a life abstainer, and my mother before me, and my husband is also, and I think this has a great deal to do with the difficulties of pregnancy. I have always been able to do my home duties, with the exception of washing, and I have not always done that. I was twenty-two years when my first baby was born. My youngest is now eleven years, and I am in my fifty-second year, and am enjoying splendid health, and am a busy woman.

Wages 24s. to 40s.; seven children.

127. Wine lodges should be closed.

I have not had or gone through so much pain and suffering as many poor mothers have to go through.

It was during pregnancy I did suffer through my own ignorance. I had a most devoted mother, and was carefully brought up, but on this subject she failed. I was the youngest of three girls, and not even my sisters, who were both married before me, did I ever hear any mention of this ... I was in my twenty-fourth year, so I was not too young to be instructed. It would have been very much better for my health if I had received some knowledge of this. I feel so glad you have given me this opportunity to just say something on the subject. I have recently visited one of our prisons, and find that the greatest number of women and girls who have fallen through drink have commenced to form this habit with it being given to them when young girls, and again when they become mothers. Of course, we know it is a weakness, but when a mother, nurse, or doctor could just as well give them many things which would do far more good for them, and save them from this. If we could only rise up in a body, we

Guildwomen, and close the wine lodges, we could save our young women! It is there where the White Slave traffic often starts, and these women will tell you. I could give you several accounts of these poor downcast creatures, but I am afraid I would be going away from the subject you are anxious to gain all information. I was in Mrs. R.'s Home for Infants yesterday, and I saw there quite enough to know what kind of mothers and fathers those babies must belong to. They do not get enough food or rest before these mites come into the world. If we could have afternoon classes for our young married women, and give them good instruction and knowledge for them to be able to be quite prepared to carry out when the time comes! We have had in our Guild this session some splendid evening lectures from doctors and nurses; but when I call round before we have these lectures and ask the young mothers to come to the meetings, they are busy with the home duties or children, so I think afternoon classes for a short time would do a great amount of good.

Wages 45s. 6d. to 60s.; one child.

128. 'Often went short of food.'

It is so long ago since I had all these babies, that I almost forget, but I was married young, and was always delicate on the chest, as I am still. I had children very fast, seven one after another, not more than a year and nine months between them, and in one case only one year and two months. Then I lost a sweet little girl, aged four years and eight months. She was ill a fortnight, and I nursed her night and day. I was so done up with attending her and the grief, that I had a dreadful miscarriage which nearly cost me my life. I had to work very hard to do everything for my little family, and after that I never had any more children to live. I either miscarried, or they were still-born. I have had two miscarriages in a year, one in January and one in August. My husband's standing wage was 28s., but he made a little overtime sometimes, which I always tried to put by for doctor and nurse. The doctor's fee was £1 1s., and I had no nurse under 1s. a day – viz., 7s. or 8s. per week, and their food, etc. I looked after my husband and children well, but I often went short of food myself, although my husband did not know it. He used to think my appetite was bad, and that I could not eat. I never worried him. He was steady, and gave me all he could. You may guess I was always scheming and planning to make ends meet, which was not good for me or the unborn baby. But I always tried to keep a bright face, and made the best of things, and all my doctors have called me plucky. I wish I had had the 30s. the mothers have now; it would have taken a load off anyhow ...

> *Wages 28s.; seven children, three still-births,*
> *four miscarriages.*

129. An agricultural labourer's wife.

I was married twenty-five years ago. My husband is an agricultural labourer, and was then earning 10s. per week, an extra shilling because he was the milkman, and went twice on Sundays. Could you afford more children on that? NO. His wages are now 15s. per week, but we are now forty-seven years old. I wish I could have had 30s. In my case it was one year's illness, nine months before and three months after. With my last I had dropsy, and was quite unable to walk for three months before baby was born. There was no money coming in, only barely enough to get bread and a small piece of butter or dripping for the four of us. You will perhaps understand we did not want any more family. We could not afford it. We love children, both of us, and often say we wish we had a larger grown-up family now we are getting into years. Our silver wedding is next Christmas.

I am by trade a leather-glove maker, my earnings helped to keep the home. The labourer of today is not so well off as we were, although they now get 16s., as food is so much dearer. With all good wishes for our nation's welfare.

Wages 10s. to 15s.; three children.

130. Ten shillings coming in for twelve weeks.

After my first-born, everything went on all right, but after my second, I was very ill with my breasts, but, of course, I put that down to my husband's lack of work. He was thrown out for twelve weeks just as baby was born, and, of course, it was a dreadful worry to me. Fancy 10s. coming in for twelve weeks, 5s. 9d. for rent out of it, and a new baby. I am not the only one, but I felt I could never have any more, as much as I love children, and now, after eleven years, the thought of it makes me feel ill. During the time of pregnancy I suffered dreadfully, and my heart goes out to all my poorer sisters, and if there is anything I can do to help in any way, I am at your service. Of course, I am far from strong, but as long as I can, I am quite willing to help.

Wages 34s. to 38s.; two children.

131. Consoled herself with an orphan boy.

I have been married thirteen years and have no children. I have had seven miscarriages, all under six months. My own opinion is that the first was brought on by an unqualified midwife that I had to call in to see me at a moment's notice, for instead of letting me lie quiet, she acted with me as though it was a full-time child. And all the other miscarriages have followed as the result of the first. My mother is a qualified midwife, but was too far away at the time. I have suffered untold agonies through these miscarriages. My health is all undermined. The doctor has told me that I would probably give birth to a full-time child, but I should have to stay in bed for the first six months. I am glad our Guild is taking up these things, for the woman's sake, for there is many a childless woman today through neglect. I have consoled myself by adopting an orphan boy, who is the sunshine of my life.

Wages 23s. to 28s.; no child, seven miscarriages.

132. 'The terrible suffering I endured.'

The first part of my life I spent in a screw factory from six in the morning till five at night; and after tea used to do my washing and cleaning. I only left two weeks and three weeks before my first children were born. After that I took in lodgers and washing, and always worked up till an hour or so before baby was born. The results are that three of my girls suffer with their insides. None are able to have a baby. One dear boy was born-ruptured on account of my previous hard work. Two of my lads, one married is a chronic sufferer, and has three children; another, the one that was ruptured, has outgrown that, but he is far from a robust lad. I can only look back now on the terrible suffering I endured, that tells a tale now upon my health. I could never afford a nurse, and so was a day or two after my confinements obliged to sit up and wash and dress the others.

My husband's wages varied owing to either hot weather or some of the other men not working. I have known him come home with £3 or £4, and I have seen him come home with *nothing*; and when earning good money, as much as 30s. has been paid away in drink. I had three little ones in two years and five months, and he was out of work two years, and during that time I took in washing and sewing, and have not been near a bed for night after night. I was either at my sewing-machine or ironing after the little ones had gone to bed. After being confined five days I have had to do all for my little ones. I worked sometimes up till a few moments before they were born. I do hope I have not done wrong in relating so much of my past, and that it may be of some use in the furthering of our scheme.

Wages £3 or £4 to nothing; ten children, two miscarriages.

133. Maternity benefit 'intended for themselves.'

I was married when nineteen years of age, and my first baby was born just nine months after, and that was before I was twenty. My second was born two years afterwards, and, owing to ignorance, I got up too soon after confinement, and it has left me with a weakness that I suffer from now. I think that a woman is anxious to get about too soon, but now that the Maternity Benefit provides for proper nursing, women should be made to understand that the money is intended for themselves. It is more knowledge and help that women need.

I hope that you will get a great amount of information on this important subject.

Wages 20s. and house; two children.

134. An awful struggle.

First child, very sick early period, and when labour set in kept it to myself; baby born before doctor arrived. Got on well.

Second, through reaching high shelf, child had to be turned, causing good deal of suffering. Child died at three months, undergoing operation for nerves. Doctor said caused by rick or strain at birth. Miscarriage caused by fright. Did not understand it; got up next day, went about usual duties.

Third child, usual symptoms. Fourth ditto. Second miscarriage, hard work and lifting bath of water, being very weak. Doctor said would have been twins. Fifth child born on stairs, no ill-effects. Third miscarriage, very ill. Sixth child very ill, caused by lifting out of bed sick child. The bladder obstructing the way, and child could not be born only by replacing it. Labour lasting from Thursday morn until Saturday noon. Seventh and eighth child quite natural.

When we were married, thirty-one years ago, my husband was a framework knitter. Having learnt his trade thoroughly, he was capable of earning from £2 to £3 weekly, but we had only been married a fortnight when, through the introduction of machinery, he was out of work. In less than two years his earnings was 11s. to 16s. weekly. Our rent was 5s. 3d., but I let the two front rooms.

The third year he was out twelve weeks, only earning 2s. 6d. the whole time. No one would employ him; he looked pale, and his hands, owing to using silk and cotton, were soft and clean. One man told him he was not the sort of man for field-work. However, he got a job as rural postman, earning 15s. a week, leaving home 5 a.m., returning 7 p.m. In order to supplement his earnings, he hired a room and mended boots, but some people did not pay him, and he had to give it up. Then a manufacturer found he could still do with a little hand-work, but alas! things were no better; some weeks he earned 20s., some weeks less.

There were five of us to keep, so I got some work from the factory, and if I worked hard I could sometimes earn 8s. I would rise at 6 a.m., get my housework done by 10 a.m., sending the two little ones to school, and, except for meals or attending to my little ones, worked till 12 p.m. I was then within a few weeks' birth of my little one, but – oh, how can I tell you! – one night on looking up from my work, my husband was looking ghastly. But that looking up saved my life; he told me after he was anticipating taking my life and my little ones' and his own. But he feared his courage would fail him before he finished. I reached my Bible from the shelf (it was my custom to read every night) and went to bed. But think of it! – a kinder, better man it would be difficult to find.

When I could not get shirt-finishing, I used to seam hose – 2¾d. for twelve pairs – and when my baby was born

I had 5s.; I gave it to the midwife. My husband had influenza, and we were both in bed ill. He had earned 8s., and I gave that to nurse and dismissed her. The ninth day I was downstairs doing some washing – sitting, of course – and I sent for some work, but could not do much, my eyes were so weak. I never thought to appeal to our friends to help us, but I wrote and told of the birth and said work was very bad.

A builder wanted a handyman, and sent for my husband, and gave him work – 20s. a week. My husband was so handy he kept him on as carpenter, and he attended continuation classes with our elder son, and from that he went to the Technical Institute, and about eight years after we came to ——, he had learned the second trade of carpenter, and gets the rate because he is trade unionist, and has been ever since he started as carpenter. It was he who tried to instil co-operative principles into me, but I think it was the 'divi' had the greatest influence, and the rest I learnt in the Guild room; and I say, God speed co-operation, the greatest blessing possible for the people. We seldom ever refer to our dark days, we are so happy now with our children. The baby No. 8 – it was all right. I could draw a £2 divi – the most I ever had for confinement.

Wages 11s. to £1; eight children, three miscarriages.

135. Rag-sorting.

Her husband was a bricklayer's labourer, and the woman did rag-sorting to help with the living, and used to wheel sacks full of rags on a sack-barrow to the warehouse. The wonder to me was that the babies were born alive, though it was never stated that it was through this that the children died soon after. My own impression was that it had something to do with it. As a mother myself I would not have dared to have attempted to do what that poor woman had to do, and I am thankful to know that something is being done to try and alleviate these poor women. As a Bible woman who visits in and out of the homes of the poor, my heart aches as I see how some of these poor women have to work during pregnancy, and how little comfort they have at the time, and how soon they have to begin work again, before they are fit, and I believe many poor women suffer for life through having to get about too soon.

Wages 23s.

136. 'I wonder how I lived.'

I do not know that my experience of child-bearing has differed much from the women of my class. I was a factory girl, and an only child. I was married at twenty, and the mother of three children by the time I was twenty-three.

I was totally ignorant of the needs of my children or how to look after myself as I should do, and now I look back, I wonder how I muddled through, for that is really what it was, a muddle all the time, and it was more by fortune than wit that I have reared my first two children to maturity.

When I look back to that first three years of my married life, I wonder how I lived through it. I was weak and ill, could not suckle my second baby. And then a third baby coming along made my life a continual drudgery, and to crown my misfortune my husband fell out of work, and I had to do shirt work at home in order to keep a roof over our heads. My third baby was very tiny and thin when born. I put this down to the worry and the shortness of food which I had to put up with, and though he lived till he was three years old and died from diphtheria. It was a happy release to me, as he was an epileptic, and I thanked God, much as I loved him, that he was taken from this life, where even sound people have a difficulty to exist.

I do not think I was very different in my pregnancies to others. I always prepared myself to die, and I think this awful depression is common to most at this time. And when bothered by several other children, and not knowing how to make ends meet, death in some cases would be welcome if it were not the dread of the children. 'How would they get on without their mother?'

My husband was fortunate enough, just after the loss of my third child, to get regular work, and I never bore another child under such awful conditions. But I believe that I felt the effects of it in all my other pregnancies.

After the first three living children, I had three stillborn children. I was six months advanced when I fell downstairs over a stair-rod, which killed the child, which was born after forty-eight hours' labour, and perhaps it seems wicked to you, but I was glad, because it left my hands free for a time to look after the other two, for I was fearfully weak and ill. After a lapse of two years I had another seven-months baby born dead, and again, after another two years, a five-months still-born child, all three still-born children being boys. I had a miscarriage after this of two months, and when I was thirty-five years old had my last baby, who is now living, nine years old.

I do hope you will not feel that this letter is morbid, and that I delight in writing horrors, for I do not, and had you not asked for information I should never have written this all down. It is strictly true, and when I look back to my early married life I could cry for the girl who endured so much for life that was wasted. I am fairly healthy now myself and have much to thank God for – a loving help-meet and dutiful children – so please do not think I am miserable, for I am not, for I believe – in fact, I know – that there is a brighter day dawning for the mother and child of the future.

Wages 21s. to 30s.; four children, three still-births, one miscarriage.

137. Five still-births.

Mine is rather an exceptional case. Through being left without a mother when a baby – father was a very large farmer and girls were expected to do men's work – I, at the age of sixteen, lifted weights that deformed the pelvis bones, therefore making confinement a very difficult case. I have five fine healthy girls, but the boys have all had to have the skull-bones taken away to get them past the pelvis. Always a case for two or three doctors, so you will know I have suffered something. I wish more could be done to train young girls to be more careful. Over my first baby I was eleven months before I could walk again. A woman ought, in my opinion, to be treated more or less as an invalid during pregnancy. I suffered most with sickness and swollen legs, terrible bad carryings. You cannot follow up with work as you ought to do. I suffered with a terrible bearing-down pain all through carrying. I often wonder how some poor women do that have such very fast confinements every twelve months and no care at all bestowed on them.

Wages 20s. to 22s. 6d.; five children and five still-births.

138. A weaver.

My first baby was born before I was twenty. I was a weaver, and worked hard until after the eighth month. I had a very hard labour, and cannot tell you very much, as I was unconscious before the baby was born. The first thing I knew was my mother standing over me trying to keep me awake. The doctor said I was not to go to sleep for two hours, or I should not waken again. The child was a big boy, and was crushed with being born and obstruction. Then inflammation took place, and he only lived four days. I was soon downstairs again and at work. I was seven years before I had another – a girl; then I had another boy. The two are now grown up, and I have said good-bye to weaving. I hope my two children will have a better time than I have had.

Wages 19s. to 23s.; three children.

139. Drugs.

I know personally of many mothers who have had very dreadful times of sickness all through the time, and others who have not been able to have the necessary food to strengthen them – some through having bad or careless husbands, others through shortness of work; and, I am sorry to say, those who have felt they would not carry children, some because of bad husbands, others because they felt they could not properly feed and clothe those they had. There are three who lost their lives, and another who has already had seven. These all took some kind of drug, and of course did the work they wanted it to do. The doctor felt sorry for this woman and could not blame her. She has had difficulty in rearing these seven. When she was able to get out, I saw her and talked seriously to her, but she said: 'Mrs ———, I will not have any more by him, and I should not have cared if I had died.' She loved her children, and has had months of sleepless nights with each of the seven. It seems to me, had Government awakened to its duty years ago, seeing to it that the mothers and children should have what was necessary, mothers would not have minded having the children, had they known each little one would be provided for. We should now have a stronger and healthier race of men and women. One does not wonder at the sickly boys and girls one meets in the streets, especially when one knows under what circumstances they were born, and how and what their mothers had to bear before they came.

140. Got up the fifth day.

I feel that we women ought to discuss this question, because working women often suffer terribly at these times with having to get up soon after confinement: I myself being a great sufferer with bad legs through getting up on the fifth day, although I had a doctor and midwife to attend me. But I lived in a place where the women and girls went to work in the mills, and could not get a woman to stay in the home, and I was often left without for many hours. When the midwife came, she advised me to have a bottle of stout and biscuits beside the bed; but I refused, because I had never taken stout, and I thought no food better than that. And I have trouble to this day with my legs. Although well cared for during the last two confinements, it has never remedied the unfortunate position of the first confinement.

Wages 30s.; three children.

141. A family of fifteen.

I have had a very large family (fifteen). Out of all these confinements I have only had my husband in work at the time twice. Several times he was sick, and other times it was hard winters, and as he was in the building trade, he could not work if very frosty or very wet, so you will see that I have known what it was to be often very short. With this result, that when my sixth child was born, my health failed, which would not have been the case if I had not had to go short. I also had so much worry, and was unable at the time of carrying the child to have any help, however poorly I felt. For a number of years I was in a very weak state of health, which the doctor said was the result of not being properly looked after.

Wages 24s. and upwards; fifteen children.

142. 'Much depends on the husband.'

I had my children several years apart. I must say that I was much better in health during pregnancy, and up to the time of the birth of the child was able to do most of my work. Kneeling, I found, was the worst thing, which I was careful to avoid, but a certain amount of exercise did me good. But it was after confinement that I had to be very careful. I could never sit up in bed for a fortnight, and it was a month or five weeks before I could come downstairs. That was the time I wanted all the nourishment I could get. Of course, there is a difference amongst women, as I know of some that suffer for months before with dropsy and various other things, then as a rule they are much better afterwards. Much depends on what kind of a husband the wife has. Worry must be a great drawback to a woman in that state. I am thankful to say my experience has not been a bad one, as all my children were healthy and strong. A woman cannot possibly get on if she has a bad, worrying husband. I think that makes a lot of difference.

Wages 36s.; four children.

143. Problem of housework.

I am bound to say that I have never had bad times, neither before nor after birth. Of course, I have tried to obey the laws of Nature, taking plenty of exercise, good plain food, avoiding constipation – all three very essential things in such cases. Also, I have had home comforts, a husband who has studied me in every respect during the time. Some women are dreadfully sick all the way through, which is much against both the child and herself. I am never sick from beginning to end. The most difficult thing at the time is securing a woman who is able and willing to do housework, and look after the woman at the same time; that to me is one of the greatest problems in the Maternity Scheme today. If something could be done to organise such women, then it would mean much. A midwife simply goes and washes the baby and sees to the mother once a day for a week, but when the mother gets up, she often has more loss, and therefore feels her weakness.

Wife's allowance 18s. to 30s.; six children, one still-born.

P.S. – I could give you many very wretched cases, as I am on the Guild of Help Committee, also the N.S.P.C.C., so come across a lot of sad cases – in fact, I have a case on my list just now where the woman has had thirteen children under fourteen years. Twelve are living, the last two being born this week. I visited her before the children were born, to see if she was having sufficient food for herself and family, as her husband was unable to work, suffering from nystagmus. She said she had only been able to eat dry toast for weeks, her throat and chest were so bad. The woman at this time is very ill, and has two babies to consider. Her husband has done nothing for ten weeks. These are the cases we want to fight for.

144. Bad medical attendance.

I have had three children. There was one year between the first and second, two years between the second and third. I have had no miscarriage, and no still-births. But I have been very ill at times ever since my children were born. I can assure you that some doctors are very neglectful at these times. This you will see when I tell you about myself at these times. My first child was a boy, and I nearly lost my life because the doctor did not bring his bag containing the necessary instruments for use at these times, and his home was five miles away. So I can assure you I was nearly gone when the child was born. Then, when I had the second one – which was a girl – the very same doctor (there was only one doctor within miles then) came nearly drunk, and I had a frightful time. What is called the after-birth had grown to my side, and he never got it all away. I had milk fever first, and then childbed fever. I lost all reason, never knew a soul for just three months. Then I had to go under an operation to have the substance got away, which left me in a very bad way, the child being eight months old when I was able to get up. And, still worse, I had nearly the same thing to go through over the third, through not being able to get a doctor, and had a midwife who was not very experienced. I had to be taken to the hospital, and the doctors told me there I should never have any more children through the way I had been treated at the last childbirth, and I was very pleased to hear it, I can assure you, after what I had gone through. My youngest child is just twenty years old, and I have never had any since, but I love children, and I think they are a blessing to every good mother. I know I shall have to suffer while I live through being neglected at childbirth. The Maternity Benefit would have been a godsend to me while I was having children.

Wages 14s. to 20s.; three children.

145. Illness costing nearly £20.

I have only had one child, a girl, and I had a most fearful time, which nearly cost me my life. I got up and tried to get about, as I had only engaged my nurse for three weeks, and I thought I must try, as time was going on, and I was in agonies all the time. The doctor had left me, and the nurse I had assured me it would pass off as I got stronger, and instead I grew worse and worse, until my husband would call in the doctor again. I had a fearful time. The womb had got twisted, and was lying on the back passage, and inflammation set in. It was worse than a confinement. What I went through! I was in bed ten weeks, and it was more than three months before I could even lift my baby or do anything. I had to be sat with day and night, and have nourishment every fifteen minutes. The woman I had to nurse me, who was recommended to me by the doctor, swarmed me with vermin, and there I was helpless. Only my husband and a neighbour to attend to my head, until the doctor sent the district nurse, and she saved my life. She was so good, and kind, and clever, one of Queen Alexandra's Nurses she was. I am so glad the Certificated Midwives are doing such grand work. We have one here in the town, and I may say she has all the cases now, and is always very busy, and is so good, and clean, and careful in the home. What we working women want today is a friend in the time of need, not a nuisance, the same as I had. It cost me nearly £20, my illness. Had it not been for our little nest-egg invested in our Co-operative Society, where should I have been? What a blessing this Maternity Benefit is! I trust I shall never require it.

Wages 27s.; one child.

146. Specialist's advice needed.

My case was rather an extraordinary one, and emphasises that the National Care of Maternity ought to be brought into force at once. Through no fault of my own, I suffered from St Vitus's dance, caused through pregnancy, and was under three local doctors, and also engaged a trained nurse, but at the last moment they decided I must go into hospital, as my case was so bad. The physician said that in a case like mine local doctors were not worth six a penny, and if I had gone to hospital at the commencement, I would never have got to the state in which I unfortunately was. The local doctors told me I could not be cured until the child was born, but the physician in hospital said it was ridiculous. If I had gone four months earlier, I could have been cured, and come home for the child to be born. I had no mother to give me advice, and the same makes me very strongly in favour of Moral Hygiene being taught in schools, so as not to leave girls ignorant of the functions of pregnancy and motherhood. Cases like mine should be brought to light in order that some poor souls in the future will be saved from going through the same as I did.

Wages 27s. 6d.; one child.

147. A small private income.

I really did not suffer much during that time, and always had good confinements. I am one of the few working men's wives who have a small private income, so I am thankful to say I have never felt the pinch.

148. 'Nine months of misery.'

I wish to give you a little on the sufferings of mothers in pregnancy. I myself might say it is a matter of nine months misery for me while I am in that condition. I might say I was married twelve months when I had my first – a little girl – and four years after we got a little boy, a fine child, born. But I had contracted a severe chill, and it was all on my chest; and having baby on the breast, it drew the cold from me, and with that took ill of catarrh of the stomach, and died at four months. Being in a weak state myself, I again found myself pregnant; but at the eight months the child was born dead, it being the second boy. Two years after I had another girl, but it was when work was slack, and my husband could get very little work, and it became so bad that we had to sell part of our home to keep ourselves, and the time I should have had extras and somebody in to look after me this was out of the question. Now, two years after, again I had another girl (my last, I hope). I might say that, although sick and ill all the time I was pregnant, I soon got over it when the time was up. I have known some poor souls go days and weeks in their labour, and then have to have instruments and chloroform, and after nearly coming to death's door have had to be stitched and syringed and doctored for months.

Wages 20s. to 22s. 6d.; five children, one still-born.

149. Every help.

I have been in the fortunate position of being able to have every help at those times, added to which my youngest child is turned twenty-six years, and time has obliterated much that I suffered at those times. My husband was earning 9d. an hour. We afterwards started in business for ourselves.

Two children, one miscarriage.

150. 'Should never have had children.'

I have not got one healthy child among my five, not because I did not get well looked after, but they are suffering through the past generation. My first child is now a man of twenty-seven, married, but has had a paralysed arm from two years old (a milder form of which was a family trouble). The second one died. My third, a daughter, is almost an invalid, through nerves, and has developed a state of 'catalepsy' whenever she is overdone. She was trained to be a shorthand typist, but is unable to follow out same, as it excites her nerves. She is now a waitress, half time, and teaches music, to enable her to keep herself. The fourth suffers from congenital heart, and is always ailing more or less. She is a dressmaker. The fifth is now nine years old, and suffers from malnutrition, and is always ailing, but a clever child for her years. We have always been able to provide everything required to keep them in good health. But in the light of the knowledge I have got since I was able to grasp what things are, I have often said I was one of the women who should never have had children, as from a girl I was always ill, right through my married life till now. I have done child-bearing, and am now in better health than I can remember. I was married when I was twenty.

Wages 35s. to 45s.; five children.

151. Systematic preparation.

I am glad you are trying to emphasise the need for *knowledge* on the part of the mother, as my own experience has proved that, given knowledge as to health and the care of the body generally before childbirth, much of the evil which now accompanies this perfectly natural thing might be avoided. In my own case, having always suffered considerably at every monthly period, and not being of a particularly robust type, I made up my mind to go into training before bringing children into the world, in order not to have to pass out at the same time, and leave them to the tender mercies of others. Accordingly, I adopted a vigorous system in order to harden the body, and soften the hip and abdomen muscles, etc. This consisted of cold sponge baths, followed by certain exercises while lying flat on a mattress. Then a rubbing of the body in sweet oil. The whole was done in ten or fifteen minutes every morning. Vegetarian diet was strictly adhered to, as this produces a cleaner, healthier child. My nurse, who laughed at all my 'fads,' remarked on the fact that the child had not the grease, etc., on it at birth which most babies have. A month before the time of birth, I left off all bone-making food such as bread, so that the birth should be easier, through the absence of very hard bones in the child. As I did not do my own housework, for exercise I walked twelve miles every day in rain, snow, etc. The baby was born in January, and the day before I took a ten-mile walk, had my cold bath, etc., and that day fortnight was out walking again, testifying plainly to the fact that a little care and attention and knowledge will work wonders, and the birth was a perfectly natural one.

Women make a great mistake in feeding overmuch at this time, and bringing fat big babies into the world. Mine were designedly small, but they made up for it after birth, and will compare favourably with any now. From the first month after birth they had cold baths, sun baths, wore one garment, only wear two coverings even in winter, sleep winter and summer in the open, never wear hats or stockings. Shoes are only worn occasionally, as they are barefooted in house and school. The eldest is in her tenth year, and neither have had anything but whooping-cough and measles when there was an epidemic of these, and they had them lightly.

Women should be taught to give up corsets, which, besides all the other evils laid to their charge, damage the nipples. I nursed both my children, and my doctor remarked on the splendid nipples I had for the purpose. This was due to the absence of corsets, and to washing them every morning in cold water, and then rubbing the breasts with oil. I have seen women with scarcely any nipples trying to feed babies, and have pitied both.

Wages of husband and wife £3 10s. to £4; two children.

152. 'Had to go out to clean and paper.'

My husband's wages have been as high as £5 a week and as low as 7s. in the winter, as they cannot work either in the rain, frost, or snow. So it means saving in summer to tide over winter. My hardest time of child-bearing was when my last one was born, it being the sixth child, all living. My husband had been out of work for eighteen weeks when there was such depression. I had to go out to clean and paper when I was six months pregnant, and I am suffering with varicose veins today as the result.

In reference to myself during pregnancy and confinements, I suffered mostly with morning sickness, swollen, aching legs, and a dragging at the left side, which has always resulted in the after-birth growing to my side, and has brought on a flooding before it could be removed, but in all my confinements I have had a qualified doctor, or I am afraid my life would have been lost.

Wages 7s. to £5; six children.

153. 'A troublesome life.'

When I was married some forty to forty-five years ago, there was no consideration as to the future conditions of wifehood and motherhood.

In business myself, after the death of my dear father, I married a business man, widower with four children. I told him when I married I would not come into the business; however, he gave me no rest until I came back. I had to care for an invalid mother, that was why I longed for a home again. I soon found out what a mistake I had made. I had my children fast. One year and five months between, and one year and seven months, and much about the same with five children. My husband was exacting as regards his children, but careless of me. I had a very happy childhood; my father was a good man, my mother a gentle creature. I lost her, and then nervous debility set in through over-strain and persecution. I lost a little girl from consumption of the bowels. I was then a wreck. I began to recover for my children's sake, but I separated from my husband, and took my four children with me, and began to make a living for myself. He provided 5s. a week for each child whilst he remained in England. He went abroad, made money, left me to struggle, and when he died, left me nothing; the money was willed to each of his and my children. By that time there were only two of mine left out of five, and four of his who received their full share. I have had a troublesome life.

In business; five children.

154. Cases of labourers' wives.

(*a*) Husband, labourer, but when at work spends most of his earnings in drink. Now four children under six years. The last one born died, aged five months, of consumption. Mother consumptive. I should say all the children are consumptive. Mother is, and I should say always has been, in a starved condition. A woman that would give the food to the children and starve herself, having always practically two babies in arms, and unable to go out to work, if she could obtain it, to bring a little money in the home. It would also be wrong to give her work, even her home duties being too much for her strength. No help wanted for the man in this case. He's too artful to starve, but wicked enough to live to continue a cause for anxiety. Nothing but food or death of husband or wife will alter this case. A sad case; a hard problem to solve.

(*b*) Husband, builder's labourer. Wife employed at laundry. Five children under eleven years of age. Husband out of work ten weeks previous to wife's confinement. During the time the home depending solely upon the wife's earnings. Wife, owing to lack of nourishment, in a very low, weak condition, and suffering much from varicose veins. Fourteen days prior to birth of child, being practically unable to stand, gave up her duties at laundry. The following day a vein burst; a very serious case. None of the previous children are very strong; but what about the last one, with the mother practically starved prior to its birth?

(c) A very similar case. Husband a labourer; work uncertain. All money he earned goes into the home. Eight children under eleven years. Woman always much underfed, owing to insufficient money coming into the home. She is never well.

155. Forty-seven nieces and nephews.

I may say that I have been fortunate in being able to have good care and a good doctor. Had I not been able to have it, I should have certainly lost my life when my still-born child was born. I was very ill for six weeks after, and I know what an expensive time it was. When I tell you that I am aunt to forty-seven nieces and nephews, all of the poor working class, you will understand that I have seen something of the struggle with poverty at such times, some having to get out and attend to the home before the child was eight days old. Knowing all this, I am out to help do all I can to hasten the day when every man, woman, and child shall have all the good things of life which is theirs by right.

Wages average £1; three children, one still-born.

156. 'A law to stay in bed ten days.'

I think there is a good deal of room for improving a mother's condition during pregnancy and after childbirth. I myself have had nothing to complain of, only ignorance in things which made me suffer more than I had any need to while I was carrying my children, being young and away from all my friends; and my mother, being one of the 'old school,' thought it wrong to talk to her girls of such things, and it always made us feel shy of asking her anything. But my youngest is now in his twelfth year. But I must say I have got a good husband, and we made that condition years ago, that as the boy grew up he would enlighten him, and I was to do the same by our girl, who is now fourteen years old. And one thing I think should be imposed on mothers is to have a doctor at confinements, and not to trust to midwives. I have seen a lot of neglect here with different people I have been with at those times. Certainly the midwife washes the mother after the birth of the child, but not again is the mother washed until she can do it herself. I think, myself, if there could be a law to make every mother have a doctor, and to stay in bed for at least ten days, and to be treated as an invalid for another fourteen days, it would save a lot of suffering. The women would get stronger, and not so liable to have children so quickly. A case in point only two doors away from me; the mother was confined on the 21st; on the 26th she was getting about her work as usual. Would a doctor have allowed that? The person is only about twenty-three years of age, and her last baby is only thirteen months old. Another case I was called in to some years ago. I did not know the person, only by sight. Her husband came and called me in the middle of the night. When I got there the child was born. No preparation had been made for either mother or child. From what I gathered, both parents had gone to bed drunk overnight. Isn't it awful, a woman getting in that state, knowing at any time she might give birth to an inno-cent little baby? It was not poverty that had brought them to that state, as the man's earnings were £2 a week, but all the man and woman had thought of was drink.

Wages 36s. to £1; two children.

157. 'Thought we must put up with it.'

I must say I have been more fortunate than some of our dear sisters. My husband always saw that I was attended to and did not want for anything. I had very bad times before and after, and was obliged to have help in for several months, and after each turn it left me with something or other. Once I lost the use of one of my hands, and the doctor said it would never get better, but however, I went to another doctor, and he cured me in a few weeks. He said it was the nerves. Our savings in the Stores have been a blessing to us, and helped us over the stile more than once. I often wondered how women could go out to work at those times, when I could not do my own. I firmly believe that if we could get better medical advice beforehand, there would not be so much suffering, and no doubt if I could have got better advice, it would have been better for me. But, of course, I thought we must put up with it, and they would only laugh at me. But however, times have altered, but too late for me.

Wages 20s. and upwards; seven children, one miscarriage.

158. Strikes, out-of-work, short time.

I have had nine children. I was two years between my first three babies. I suffered least from these three, but for about six weeks before birth, and six after, I could scarcely get about – pains all over, with a very bad back, and very much swollen legs and feet. Being a little, light-made woman, my confinements were very severe.

My fourth baby died when six weeks old – a cross-birth. Was much torn in consequence, so had to be stitched a good deal; was bad, and could scarcely get about at two months after. Neither before for weeks, nor after, could I have offered to have washed, baked, or done any work of any moment. Every confinement after this I got worse and worse. The same thing happened. Very sick for three or four months before confinement, pains all over, very bad back, legs and feet very much swollen; could not lie in bed long at a time, could get very little rest or sleep; impossible to wash, bake, or do much housework. But had a very good husband, who helped me all he could, and some sisters who came in turn and did as much as they could in my home for me. My husband's wages were very small at times, sometimes only 18s. a week, other times £1 a week, and up to 30s. In my husband's trade wages is very much up and down. Then we had a strike of eleven weeks, then short time for five months, then out of work fifteen weeks; and when one of my children was born three weeks, then over two years working four days per week. So you see there was not much money to get nourishment with. That all happened during the time I was having my children, so of course I was pretty put to sometimes. I could not have afforded to get anyone in the house if I had had to pay them all the time that I needed them, but had to prepare for a nurse each time, as I had to have one for a month at least, and after that month my sisters help. We had to do the best we could.

My last two confinements I was not able to come downstairs for about three and four months – no strength to walk, no appetite, and with being so much torn had then to come downstairs for a long time on my hips (slide down, as it were). When able to get about, could scarcely walk owing to my condition.

Wages 18s. to 30s.; nine children.

159. Rest and good food.

I have been one of those fortunate individuals who, during pregnancy, have very good health. My greatest suffering was caused by varicose veins, which, of course, are very painful at such times.

I was blessed with a good mother, who gave me good advice on the necessity of taking care of myself during this period, and having also the best of attention at confinement, and plenty of rest and good food, neither of these being lacking. I can only imagine a woman's feelings under different conditions.

My confinements (five) were, however, hard, bad times, brought about by some obstruction. This I have always put down to the fact that at the age of thirteen I began to learn dressmaking, which entailed sitting long hours at a stretch, at a time when the bones were in rather a soft state. A midwife whom I had engaged as nurse during my last confinement quite agreed that this was most likely. I could not say whether this is common among dressmakers or not.

After confinement always seemed to me to be one's weak time, and especially with nursing mothers with fine, healthy babies. I nursed four, the last being stillborn, and always found that about three months after their birth my strength failed, and doctor's advice had to be sought, when with tonics he managed to bring me right.

You see my experience will not be of much use to you, but this is exactly how I have felt during these times; in fact, during pregnancy it was much harder for me to be still than to work hard physical work.

Wages just under £2; four children, one still-born.

160. 'Eight to keep on eleven shillings and threepence.'

In the first place, being short of money is one cause of suffering. I am the mother of five children, three girls and two boys. I have not had a doctor to any of my confinements, but nearly lost my life and child's through the first one. The midwife was a qualified woman, but addicted to drink (which I found out afterwards). I was confined on a Thursday at 2.30 p.m., after many hours of suffering, and she never came near me again until late on Saturday night. Fancy me! Oh, the horror of it makes me shiver when I think about it. We were almost strangers where we were living. I had my mother staying with me, but the night before baby was born, she chopped the end of her finger right off, which made her feel very bad. She was in pain herself, and I was ignorant of the danger I was in, not being properly attended to. Mother was afraid of blood-poisoning. My husband was working nights at the time. We, like many more, had not got a very good start. He fell out of work about two months after we were married, and was out for a long time. I had to go to my home and he his, for from the first months of pregnancy I suffered greatly. When he started and worked again, I had to part with my machine (which I had paid for before I was married) to pay for rent; it was hard lines. Then he got work back, so we had to move back again – another expense. So you will see we had our trouble when baby was born. I had hardly got enough of anything, let alone doctor's money. I paid the nurse 7s. 6d. I had only been confined barely three weeks when my husband was out of work again. The first Saturday night I went out shopping after baby was born, I had 1s. 7½d. to get meat, grocery, and all else to live on till some kind friend came along, which was my mother, her home being near. She brought me a little rent, and a few shillings to carry us on for a week or two. I was afraid to spend any till my husband got work, which was after many tramps from place to place. I managed to get some work to do, but caught a cold and chill, which caused me to have a gathered breast, which nearly killed me. I did not know my own for days. They took me over from —— to ——, and thought I should die on the way there. My father soon had a doctor to see me. He told them it would be a struggle to pull me through, but after a time I gained strength to go back to ——, and as my husband had got work again, he needed me at home. Then after a year and ten months, my baby girl was born. I should tell you I was twenty-eight years old when I was married, and I had been married eleven months when my first baby was born, and I can truthfully say I was ignorant of anything concerning married life or motherhood when I was married. In fact, when the midwife came to me when I was in such pain, I had not the slightest idea where or how the child would come into the world. And another thing, I was not even told what to expect when I was leaving girlhood – I mean the monthly courses. I often wonder I got along as well as I have. I will say here that I do not intend my daughters to be so innocent of natural courses. I feel it is unkind of parents to leave girls to find these things out. It causes unnecessary suffering. I often wonder, when I hear some of our women grumbling about the trouble and bother of signing and getting the papers filled in for the 30s., how they would have been in my place, and how thankful I should have been for it.

When my girlie was eighteen months, I had a baby boy. I did think I had a handful; they seemed three babies. A friend of mine had the little girl till I got up again, which was generally ten days. Oh, what rest is there for a woman when money is so scarce? They say, 'Don't worry.' Well, what can you do? Well, I got over No. 3 fairly well, as I had a young woman to look after me for *one* week. I forgot to tell you, the day after No. 2 was born, my husband was sent away to work, so I did not see him again till she was ten days old, and I had to borrow money to get along with till he did come back. When No. 4 was born, I had a trying time. Six weeks before she was born, my three children were down with scarlet fever; two had it very badly, but the one only very slightly; they came downstairs on the Sunday for the first time. Then my baby was born the following Tuesday. The children were not allowed to see me, but the father had to look after them a good deal, as I had his young sister to look after me. I got up on the tenth day, and then my husband had the fever. We were both ill in bed together. Then I had another gathered breast. The doctor lanced it, and it ran for fourteen weeks after. Then I had a whitlow on my right thumb. During the time my husband was ill, my young sister, though she was married, came to help to look after us all. I only had 11s. 3d. a week to keep eight of us on; can you wonder a woman's strength gives way? I must also say my husband was not in a doctor's club, so we had a bill to pay for him. I and the children are in a friendly sisters' club, but the doctor does not attend confinements; that is a separate item. So you see I have known a bit of trouble. When No. 5 was born my oldest girl and boy had to look after me. The other two were sent away, one to ——, the other to ——. I had 26s. a week to keep and clothe, pay rent, fire and light, and clubs for seven of us, till my oldest started work.

I think if I had been able to have a doctor at the first I might not have suffered as I have, and do at present, as I had occasion to be examined once, and my doctor told me I had been neglected at my confinement. Oh, I do feel sometimes, if I could only tell some of the young girls things they ought to know, how much better some might be; but we have got such a class to deal with. The young girls who have babies, they only laugh at us if we say anything. I do feel one cannot be too careful about one's thoughts and actions during pregnancy; therefore, if one has not enough to live on, and get necessary life comforts, it naturally tells on the child and mother's life, as childbearing is such a strain, especially when they come so close to one another. What can a woman do but worry, when she knows there is so little to live on. I hope you do not think ill of my husband through me complaining. He has given me all the money he earned, and I have done my best – at least, I think so. I have had to fare hard and work hard; I don't know what the reward will be. —— is not like a town. There is nothing here but the pits for the boys, and the girls have to go away from home to earn a living.

I think if it had not been for the Women's Guild I should have been in the asylum. It has helped me along. I was the first member made after the Committee was formed. I was secretary for over four years. Home duties were the cause of my resigning, but I never miss a meeting. I have only missed four times since I joined. I would not miss my Guild for anything but illness. I am pleased we are to have Moral Hygiene Classes. We are having a speaker on the subject a fortnight to-morrow.

I hope I have not taken too much of your valuable time in reading this. I am suffering today through my first being not properly attended to – at least, I think so; but that was because I had no means of paying a doctor, as they expect their fee, whether anything else is paid or not. I thank Lloyd George for maternity benefit, but I do wish the wife and mother could have been insured. Who works harder than us mothers? I often say we work twenty out of twenty-four hours very often. Some days I don't sit down hardly to snatch a mouthful of food. There seems no time for women, but the men make time. If we did, we should have to be a day behind, and we don't get much Sunday rest. I am forty-eight now, so I hope I'll have no more.

Wages 17s. to 25s.; five children.

METHOD OF INQUIRY

The following questions, with a short letter, were sent to about 600 members who were, or had been, officials of the Women's Co-operative Guild, of whose family histories nothing was previously known. The letter asked these members to bring out in their replies what they 'have felt about the difficulty of taking care, the ignorance that has prevailed on the conditions of pregnancy, and how these conditions result in lack of health and energy, meaning that a woman cannot do justice to herself or give her best to her husband and children.'

The questions asked were:

1. How many children have you had?
2. How soon after each other were they born?
3. Did any die under five years old, and if so, at what ages and from what causes?
4. Were any still-born, and if so how many?
5. Have you had any miscarriages, and if so how many?

Replies were received from 386 Guild members, covering 400 cases, a few of which were not those of members of the Guild.

A second letter was sent later, asking for particulars of wages and the occupation of the husband. The wages given at the end of the letters represent as far as possible the actual amount received, not the rate of wages.

Of these letters, 160 are published. The remainder describe similar conditions.

Out of the total number of the cases, at least two-thirds indicate conditions of maternity which are not normal and healthy.

OCCUPATIONS OF HUSBANDS

Agricultural labourer.
Asylum attendant.

Baker.
Blacksmith.
Boat-builder.
Boiler-maker.
Boot operative.
Blast-furnace man.
Brass finisher.
Bricklayer.
Brush finisher.

Cabinet-maker.
Carpenter and joiner.
Carpet weaver.
Cartwright.

Carriage-maker.
Chef.
Civil servant.
Clerk.
Cloth puller.
Coachman.
Colliery workers:
　　Banksman.
　　Coal-tipper.
　　Engineer.
　　Joiner.
　　Machine clerk.
　　Miner.
　　Official.
Cooper.
Cotton-spinner.
Cycle-maker.

Diamond worker.
Dyeing and cleaning
worker.

Electrician.
Electro-plate worker.
Engineer.
Engineer's fitter.
Engine-fitter.

Foundry worker.
Framework-knitter.

Gardener.

Insurance agent.
Iron-miner.
Iron-moulder.
Iron worker.

Jewel-case maker.

Labourer.
Laundry manager.
Leather worker.
Lift-man.
Lithographer.

Loom-mender.

Machine-fitter.
Motor mechanic.
Municipal fireman.

Naval artificer.
Naval schoolmaster.
Naval seaman.
Navvy.
Nurseryman.

Painter.
Paperhanger.
Plasterer.
Plumber.
Plumber's labourer
Policeman.
Postal employee
Potter.
Printer.

Quarryman.

Railway workers:
    Engine-driver.
    Porter.

Signalman.
Telegraph clerk.
Road foreman.
Rope-maker.

Sailor.
Scientific instrument-
   maker.
Screw-maker.
Shaper.
Sheet-metal worker.
Shipwright.
Shipyard-plater.
Shop assistant.
Shopkeeper.
Silk worker.
Silversmith.
Stoker.
Stonemason.
Stonemason's labourer.

Tailor.
Tape-sizer.
Teacher.
Telegraph labourer.
Timberyard worker.
Tin-box maker.

Tinplate worker.
Tool-maker.

Waggon-builder.
Warehouseman.
Watchmaker.
Weaver.
Whitesmith.
Wood-cutting machinist
Wood-turner.

FIGURES BEARING ON INFANT MORTALITY

Still-births and miscarriages.

In collecting the letters, the object was not to obtain accurate statistics, but a general picture of the conditions of life during the period of maternity. It is, however, possible to give fairly accurate figures showing the proportions of the number of still-births, miscarriages, and deaths from pre-natal causes and injuries at birth, to the number of live births.

Of the 400 cases, 26 were childless, and 26 did not give definite figures. The number of families to which the following figures refer is therefore 348.

Total number of live births, 1,396.

Number of miscarriages, 218 (15.6 per 100 live births).

Number of still-births, 83 (5.9 per 100 live births).

Total of still-births and miscarriages, 301 (21.5 per 100 live births).

Of the 348 mothers, 148 (42.4 per cent) had still-births or miscarriages. Twenty-two had both still-births and miscarriages, 37 had still-births, 89 had miscarriages. Of the 111 women who had miscarriages (including 22 who had still-births also) –

2 women had 10 miscarriages each.

1 woman had 8 miscarriages.

1 woman had 7 miscarriages.

3 women had 6 miscarriages each.

2 women had 5 miscarriages each.

6 women had 4 miscarriages each.

9 women had 3 miscarriages each.

17 women had 2 miscarriages each.

70 women had 1 miscarriage each.

Of the 52 women who had still-births (including 22 who had miscarriages also) –

1 woman had 5 still-births.

1 woman had 4 still-births

3 woman had 5 still-births each

9 woman had 2 still-births each

45 woman had 1 still-birth each

Infant Deaths.

Total number of live births, 1,396.

Total number of deaths under 1 year, 122 (8.7 per 100 live births).

Of the 122 deaths, 26 took place in the first week of life, 12 between the first week and first month, and 23 later, owing to ante-natal causes or injury at birth.

Thus, 50 per cent of the deaths occurred either within the first month or from ante-natal or natal causes after the first month.

Of the 348 mothers, 86 (24.7 per cent) lost children in the first year of life.

LOCAL GOVERNMENT BOARD MEMORANDUM

Maternity and Child Welfare.

A complete scheme would comprise the following elements, each of which will, in this connection, be organised in its direct bearing on infantile health:

1. Arrangements for the local supervision of Midwives.

2. Arrangements for—
Ante-Natal
(1) An ante-natal clinic for expectant mothers.
(2) The home visiting of expectant mothers.
(3) A maternity hospital or beds at a hospital, in which complicated cases of pregnancy can receive treatment.

3. Arrangements for—
Natal
(1) Such assistance as may be needed to ensure the mother having skilled and prompt attendance during confinement at home.

(2) The confinement of sick women, including women having contracted pelvis or suffering from any other condition involving danger to the mother or infant, at a hospital.

4. Arrangements for—
Post-Natal

(1) The treatment in a hospital of complications arising after parturition, whether in the mother or in the infant.

(2) The provision of systematic advice and treatment for infants at a baby clinic or infant dispensary.

(3) The continuance of these clinics and dispensaries, so as to be available for children up to the age when they are entered on a school register – *i.e.*, the register of a public elementary school, nursery school, crèche, day nursery, school for mothers or other school.

(4) The systematic home visitation of infants and of children not on a school register as above defined.

LOCAL GOVERNMENT BOARD, WHITEHALL S.W.
July, 1914.

SUMMARY OF
THE NOTIFICATION OF BIRTHS
(EXTENSION) ACT, 1915

The main provisions of the Act having reference to England and Wales are:

1. That the notification of births and still-births is made compulsory in all cases.

2. That the powers of Sanitary Authorities for dealing with maternity and infancy are extended to County Councils.

3. That a Committee or Committees may be set up for exercising these powers, which must include women and may include other than members of the Authority.

The clause referring to this committee reads as follows: 'Any such powers may be exercised in such manner as the Authority direct by a committee or committees, which shall include women, and may comprise, if it is thought fit, persons who are not members of the Authority. Any such committee may be empowered by the Authority by which it is appointed to incur expenses up to a limit for the time being fixed by the Authority, and, if so empowered, shall report any expenditure by them to the Authority in such manner and at such times as the Authority may direct. A committee appointed for the purposes of this section shall hold office for such period, not exceeding three years, as the Authority by which it is appointed may determine.'

As regards Scotland and Ireland, the powers conferred are considerably larger, as the Local Authority 'within the meaning of the principal Act may make such arrangements as they think fit, and as may be sanctioned by the Local Government Board for Scotland (or Ireland), for attending to the health of expectant mothers and nursing mothers, and of children under five years of age within the meaning of Section 7 of the Education (Scotland) Act, 1908.'

The clause as regards administration by committees including women applies also to Scotland and Ireland.

NOTIFICATION OF BIRTHS
(EXTENSION) ACT, 1915

LOCAL GOVERNMENT BOARD,
WHITEHALL, S.W.
July 29, 1915.

Sir,

I am directed by the Local Government Board to bring to the notice of the Council the provisions of the Notification of Births (Extension) Act, 1915, which has recently been passed.

The objects of this Act are to make universal throughout the country the system of the Notification of Births Act, 1907, under which early information concerning all births is required to be given to the medical officer of health, and also to enable local authorities to make arrangements for the care of mothers, including expectant mothers, and young children.

At a time like the present the urgent need for taking all possible steps to secure the health of mothers and children and to diminish ante-natal and post-natal infant mortality is obvious, and the Board are confident that they can rely upon local authorities making the fullest use of the powers conferred on them.

Notification of Births Act, 1907,
to extend to every District.

The Act provides that on and after the first of September next the Notification of Births Act, 1907, described as the principal Act, shall extend to and take effect in every area in which it is not already in force.

In the case of a county district the principal Act will come into operation as if it had been adopted by the Council of the urban or rural district.

The principal Act provides that in the case of every child born within the district it is the duty of the father of the child, if he is actually residing in the house where the birth takes place at the time of its occurrence, and of any person in attendance upon the mother at the time of, or within six hours after, the birth, to give notice in writing of the birth to the medical officer of health of the district. This notice must be given in the case of every child which has issued forth from its mother after the expiration of the twenty-eighth week of pregnancy whether alive or dead.

The notice is to be given by prepaid letter or postcard addressed to the medical officer of health, giving the necessary information of the birth within thirty-six hours after the birth, or by delivering a written notice of the birth at the office or residence of the medical officer within the same time. The local authority is required to supply without charge addressed and stamped postcards containing the form of notice to any medical practitioner or midwife residing or practising in their area who applies for the same.

The Act also provides for penalties for failure to notify a birth in accordance with the Act.

It will be the duty of every local authority in whose area the principal Act comes into force by virtue of the new Act to bring the provisions of the principal Act to the attention of all medical practitioners and midwives practising in the area [Section 1 (3)].

The Board wish especially to call attention to section 1 (2) of the new Act, under which the medical officer of a county district, for which the principal Act had not previously been adopted, will be required to send duplicates of any notices of birth he receives to the county medical officer of health as soon as may be after they are received. The early receipt of these duplicate notices is important, particularly in facilitating the inspection of midwives, and the Board trust that arrangements will be made under which the duplicates are as a matter of routine immediately transmitted to the county medical officer.

Administrative Arrangements under the Act.

Section 2 of the Act provides that for the purpose of following up the information obtained under the powers of the principal Act and for facilitating arrangements for the care of expectant mothers, nursing mothers and young children, all the powers of the Public Health Acts may be exercised. These powers will be available not only to all sanitary authorities, but also to all County Councils other than the London County Council. In London the powers of the Public Health (London) Act, 1891, will be available for work undertaken in regard to the care of mothers and young children by Metropolitan Borough Councils.

It will be seen, therefore, that the Act definitely contemplates that the powers of sanitary authorities will be used to promote the care of mothers and young children.

The Board are anxious to insist on the importance of linking up this work with the other medical and sanitary services provided by local authorities under the Public Health and other Acts. They have already in their circular letter of the 30th July, 1914, on the subject of Maternity and Infant Welfare, indicated generally the scope of the work which they consider should be undertaken, and an additional copy of that letter is enclosed.

As indicated above, the Act contemplates that arrangements for attending to mothers and young children may be made either by County Councils or by sanitary authorities. The Board recognise that the organisation must vary to some extent with local conditions, and that a considerable degree of elasticity is necessary. They are, however, of opinion that it will generally be desirable to formulate comprehensive schemes for counties and county boroughs, although in some cases portions of the services may be undertaken by the larger District Councils with advantage. The councils of counties and county boroughs are the local supervising authorities under the Midwives Act, 1902, and they are also entrusted with the initiation and execution of schemes for the treatment of tuberculosis; if the organisation of a maternity and infant welfare scheme is also undertaken by them, it will be practicable to secure the unification of home visiting for a number of different purposes.

In all cases, however, in which a general scheme is organised for the county, the work should be carried on in close co-operation with the sanitary authority, and any insanitary conditions found by health visitors should at once be reported to the sanitary authority. Although the Board consider that general schemes should be organised for the county as a whole, and that the County Council should, as a general rule, provide for health visiting, they are prepared, in suitable cases, to recognise the sanitary district as a proper area for a scheme.

Co-operation with Medical Practitioners and Voluntary Agencies.

In the development of general schemes the Board desire that the services of hospitals and other efficient voluntary agencies should be fully utilised. They are also anxious that the co-operation of medical practitioners should be secured. The value of a Maternity Centre will be much increased by obtaining the cooperation of the medical practitioners in the area to be served by it, and in organising the arrangements it is desirable that they should be consulted.

London.

In London the Act contemplates that schemes should be organised by the Metropolitan Borough Councils. Many of the services required can be provided by the various London hospitals and the numerous voluntary agencies now at work, and in some cases the chief need is to secure that such services are properly linked up with the work of the Borough Council. In other areas existing medical services will require supplementing and extending, and it will be for the Borough Councils to consider how this can best be done.

Grants in Aid of Local Expenditure.

The Government have agreed to provide, by means of annual grants to be distributed by the Board, one-half the cost of the whole or any part of schemes for maternity and child welfare approved by the Board. The regulations under which these grants will be paid, together with forms of application for grants, have already been distributed to local authorities. A further copy of the regulations is enclosed.

Interim Schemes.

Many local authorities have already prepared and submitted to the Board schemes for Maternity and Infant Welfare, embracing some or all of the items included in the Board's memorandum of 30th July, 1914. The initiation of a complete scheme, however, involves time, and the Board do not desire that work should be delayed until a complete scheme can be formulated. They trust that those local authorities who have not already taken steps in this matter will do so before the onset of the hot weather, which brings with it special dangers to infants and children. The Board are of opinion that the local authority should in the first instance carefully consider whether the existing arrangements for home visitation are adequate. After the provision of health visitors the next step should be to arrange in populous centres for a Maternity Centre at which medical advice and treatment may be provided for mothers, including expectant mothers, and for children, whether ailing or not. Arrangements should also be made for defraying in necessitous cases the cost of providing the services of a midwife and of a doctor. The Board will be prepared to sanction such provision under Section 133 of the Public Health Act, 1875.

Present Need for Maternity and Infant Welfare Work.
The importance of conserving the infant life of the population makes it desirable that steps should be taken in the directions indicated even at the present time when strict economy is required in the expenditure both of public bodies and of private individuals. It is not, however, intended that any large outlay should be involved in the provision of the services mentioned. No capital expenditure is needed, and the maintenance expenditure need not be heavy. The health visitors and many of the doctors required to work such a scheme will be women, and no labour need be employed which is required for the more direct purposes of the war.

Committees.
The Act provides that the powers of a local authority may be exercised in such manner as the authority direct by a committee or committees, which shall include women, and may comprise, if it is thought fit, persons who are not members of the authority.

In any such committee it will be desirable to include working women, who might with advantage be representative of women's organisations. Where no local women's organisation exists, some central organisation might possibly assist by suggesting suitable women.

The Board consider that on any committee appointed for the purposes of the Act there should be a majority of direct representatives of the Council.

> I am, Sir,
> > Your obedient Servant,
> > > H.C. MONRO,
> > > > *Secretary.*

ADMINISTRATIVE POWERS OF
LOCAL AUTHORITIES

The powers of County Councils* and Sanitary Authorities – *i.e.*, County Borough and Borough Councils, Urban and Rural District Councils – for maternity and infancy work are derived from the following Acts:

1. Public Health Acts, 1875-1907.
2. Midwives Act, 1902.
3. Notification of Births Acts, 1907–1915.*
4. The Milk and Dairies (Consolidation) Act, 1915.
   (This Act will not come into force till after the war.)

The following Maternity and Infancy work (with the exception of the supervision of midwives) may be carried

*See Summary of the Notification of Births (Extension) Act, 1915, on p. 225.

out by special Maternity Sub-Committees (which must include women) of the above authorities: –

Notification of Births

Every birth has to be notified in every area to the Medical Officer of Health for that area by the father of the child or the medical practitioner or midwife within thirty-six hours of the birth.

Women Sanitary Inspectors and Health Visitors.

Properly trained and qualified women may be appointed to visit the homes and give advice on the care of mothers and infants.

Maternity Centres.

Skilled advice and minor treatment for the preservation of health may be given at Maternity Centres to expectant and nursing mothers and children up to school age.

Supervision of Midwives.

County Councils and County Borough Councils alone carry out the supervision of midwives, through the Medical Officer of Health, who almost invariably has under him a fully qualified woman.

Professional Attendance at Confinements.

A doctor or midwife may be provided to attend necessitous cases. The fee of a doctor called in under the Midwives Act may be paid.

Maternity Hospitals for Complicated Cases and Infant Hospitals.

Hospitals may be maintained or beds paid for in existing hospitals or wards.

Milk Depots.

After the war, depots may be set up by Sanitary Authorities (only) for the sale of milk for infants at cost price. (The Government grant is not available for these depots.)

Government Grants.

Government grants for maternity and child welfare work are now made, and half the cost of the whole or any part of schemes, approved by the Local Government Board, is now paid.

A sum of £50,000 has been voted this year (1915) for England and Wales, and no doubt corresponding sums will be available for Scotland and Ireland.

NATIONAL SCHEME PROPOSED BY THE
WOMEN'S CO-OPERATIVE GUILD

To insure effective care of Maternity and Infancy, it would be necessary to combine the administration of benefits under the Insurance Act with the services organised by the Public Health Authority.

Maternity and Pregnancy Sickness Benefits. – These should be taken out of the Insurance Act, extended to all women (under the income-tax limit), and increased in amount. In addition to the 30s. maternity benefit, every mother should receive £3 10s. in weekly payments of 10s. for three weeks before and four weeks after confinement (or for longer periods if she prefers smaller weekly payments). During pregnancy she should be entitled to benefit varying according to her condition, from 2s. 6d. to 7s. 6d. a week, if her health requires it, subject to the recommendation of a maternity centre or a doctor.

Public Health Authorities should be empowered to

administer these benefits through women health officers and maternity centres.

Notification of Births. – Notification of births and still-births is now compulsory throughout the country, and in order to make it effective, an adequate number of Health Visitors should be appointed in every area.

Women Health Officers. – The status of Health Visitors should be raised, their salaries being increased, and three qualifications being required – *i.e.*, midwifery, sanitary, and nursing certificates.

Midwifery and Nursing. – These services should be organised by the Public Health Authorities, which already supervise midwives. Longer training for midwives should be required, and an adequate salary secured to them by the Public Health Authorities. A charge of 10s. might be made to mothers employing them, to be remitted if the circumstances require it. This is the only method of meeting the present shortage of midwives, which is particularly serious in rural districts. It is also the only way of securing skilled attention for the women at a charge within their reach, and at the same time of securing adequate payment for midwives. Municipal midwives could be employed with a doctor.

The administration of the Treasury grant for nursing should also be placed under the Public Health Authority.

Maternity and Infant Centres. – These centres should be places where expectant and nursing mothers and children up to school age can come for advice and treatment, so that they may be kept well and made well. Their organisation will depend on local circumstances, but it will be found desirable in most cases to open several centres, so that they may be near the people's homes and serve the different classes of women in different localities.

Advice to expectant mothers might be given either at local maternity centres or at centres at hospitals.

It is important that treatment of a simple nature should be given with advice at maternity centres. Nourishment being often the treatment mothers most need, provision should be made for dinners for expectant and nursing mothers when ordered by the doctor. Simple talks on personal hygiene, infants' clothing, etc: should be arranged, and saving-clubs organised.

Medical Service. – It is desirable to appoint women doctors as municipal officers of the centres, but local practitioners may in some cases be advantageously worked into a municipal scheme. The provision of a doctor called in under the Midwives Act should be part of the scheme.

Maternity Hospitals or Beds. – The dearth of such hospitals for abnormal cases is calamitous. The need for their existence is also pressing from the point of view of research, and they could be used as training schools for doctors and midwives.

Maternity Homes. – These are required for normal cases. The few voluntary homes in existence in England are most valuable, and the experience of New Zealand shows that municipal homes could be made self-supporting. Private doctors might attend their patients in the homes.

Milk Depots. – The difficulties of securing pure milk make it desirable to establish municipal depots for the supply of milk to expectant and nursing mothers and children. While every precaution should be taken not to undermine the practice of breast-feeding, there are cases where specially prescribed bottles would be useful.

Household Helps. – The need for help in the home before, at, and after confinement is urgent, but in order to prevent untrained women doing midwifery work, careful supervision and an organised service under the public health authority are necessary. The experiments made by relief committees show the value of such a service.

Women as Councillors. – Working women should be elected on to councils and serve on public health committees.

Public Health Maternity Sub-Committees. – These committees should be largely composed of representatives of the women concerned. Such representation should be secured whenever possible through the following industrial women's organisations: the Women's Co-operative Guild, Women's Trade Unions, the Women's Labour League, and the Railway Women's Guild.

Any parts of this scheme not at first taken over by Public Health Committees – *e.g.*, Dinners, Household

Helps – might be organised experimentally by the sub-committees with a view to ultimate inclusion in a municipal scheme.

Ministry of Health. – In the future it will probably be advantageous to establish a Ministry of Health, with a Maternity and Infant Life Department, partly staffed by women.

It is essential that Government departments and Public Health Committees should be in constant communication with organised working-women, and be ready to welcome their co-operation, so that their needs and wishes may be freely consulted. It is by a partnership between the women who are themselves concerned, the medical profession, and the State that the best results of democratic government can be secured for the mothers and infants of the country.

To be obtained from the Women's Co-operative Guild, 28, Church Row, Hampstead, London, N.W.:

The National Care of Maternity (leaflets for town and country), ½d. each, or 3s. a hundred.

Hints to Expectant Mothers, by Dr J. W. Ballantyne, price 1d., or 6s. a hundred.

Household Helps, ½d. each, or 3s. a hundred.

AFTERWORD

By Gloden Dallas

'Do publish these letters ... they are so amazing' wrote Virginia Woolf to her friend Margaret Llewelyn Davies, General Secretary of the Women's Co-operative Guild from 1889 until 1921. The letters, one hundred and sixty of them, written by Guild members and telling of childbirth and death, exhaustion and self-sacrifice, of totally inadequate pre-natal care, of poverty, abortion, sometimes despair, form the matter of this book.

The Guild had begun in 1883 with the modest aims of giving the wives of male co-operators an interest in the movement, and of encouraging them, mainly in their role as consumers, towards some form of independent self expression. In the years before the First World War, it had developed under Miss Davies' tutelage into a vigorous campaigning organization of some 32,000 working women. The letters in *Maternity* were sent in 1914 in response to an appeal from Miss Davies for direct experiences of childbirth and rearing to be used as evidence in the Guild's sustained campaign against the Liberal government and local authorities, to improve the virtually non-existent maternal and infant care then available to the poorer woman.

Pressure from the Guild had helped to secure the inclusion of thirty shillings maternity benefit in Lloyd George's National Insurance Act, and in 1913, after 'a lightning campaign', the benefit was accepted as legally the property of the mother. These victories, though of great importance, did not reach the heart of the problem. The negligent medical care, poor feeding, ignorance and overwork, well known to Miss Davies and the Guild, were revealed to a wider public in this book.

Whether the letters were originally intended for publication or for petition is not clear – the subject matter was, for its time, not only amazing but almost unmentionable – but in February 1915 the Woolfs, on Miss Davies' behalf, sent them to Gerald Duckworth, Virginia's half-brother and publisher of her early works. Duckworth's did not publish, but the letters did appear in September of the same year, at two shillings and sixpence a copy, under the imprint of G. Bell and Sons.

Public reaction to the book was highly favourable. *The Times* gave a 'very warm review' and the *Times Literary Supplement* said 'A book of notable interest and of singular distinction has just been published on the distresses, hardships, sufferings and enfeeblement which poverty and maternity, between them, inflict upon women. This book is thoroughly original, thoroughly first-hand.'

Bell's, for their part, claimed that no book they had issued in years had been so widely and so favourably received. Margaret Llewelyn Davies merely wrote that 'the book made a great effect in Britain and America'. It was almost immediately sold out on first edition – partly due to a recommendation, in extra heavy type, in the Women's Corner of the *Co-operative News* for October 2 1915, that 'every branch should buy a copy ... and it might be lent out to your members at ½d or 1d a week'. By November, a second edition was printed and selling.

For Guild members, *Maternity* was, if not the culmination, certainly the public revelation of the unpalatable facts which lay behind their pressure on the authorities, and their encouragement of local self help amongst women. The reforms demanded ranged from the provision of fully equipped maternity and infant welfare centres, free extra nutrition for needy mothers, through to the establishment of home help services and 'pure milk' depots – the details are listed meticulously by Miss Davies in an appendix to this book. Many such services were already within the power of local authorities and the Guild used the opportunity of wartime to urge the central authorities to pressurize local councils and health authorities to use their powers.

Miss Davies, herself a pacifist, accepted that more attention was likely to be paid to the mothers of the 'nation's assets' at a time when the nation regarded them as potential future soldiers and workers. 'The Local Government Board offices were crowded with mothers and their babies, an unusual sight for Whitehall. They came to ask Herbert Samuel to recognize that, during the war, maternity was more important than ever.'

Herbert Samuel gave such recognition, partly on humanitarian grounds, partly because, as he said, without action to protect the mothers 'the nation is weakened. Numbers are of importance. In the competition and conflict of civilizations, it is the mass of the nation that tells.' As a result, both in 1914 and 1915, strongly worded circulars were sent out by the Local Government Board that local authorities should instigate schemes to help mothers. But many were dilatory, and Guild members kept up pressure at local level on an impressive scale. The Guild Congress report for March 1915–March 1916 notes resolutions sent to local authorities in thirty-three towns. Accrington, enterprisingly, had held 'a maternity and infant welfare week', and in twenty-six towns, schemes including the establishment of health centres, appointment of health visitors and arrangements for confinements had been adopted. Local Guild officials gave talks on preparation for maternity, and various pamphlets: *A Municipal Maternity Centre*, *What Public Health Authorities*

Can Do, *Work of a Maternity Centre*, and *Home Helps* – all one penny each – were distributed through branches.

If the needs of the state brought partial recognition to the Guild's demands, without Margaret Llewelyn Davies these demands would never have been so forcefully articulated, nor the Guild itself have become a campaigning body of national importance.

Miss Davies was born in 1861 into an upper class family much influenced by the teachings of Christian Socialism, and committed to the reform of the social conditions of late Victorian England. After an unusually good education for a woman of her day – Queen's College, London followed by Girton, Cambridge – her own early experience of the misery caused by social deprivation was gained as a sanitary inspector in St Marylebone and later through the St Marylebone branch of the Women's Guild. When she was elected General Secretary of the Guild in 1889, her father, an Anglican rector, moved to a living in the north of England, and for many years the Guild was run from the unlikely headquarters of Kirkby Lonsdale Vicarage.

Leonard Woolf, who knew her well, described Miss Davies as 'one of the most eminent women I have known', and attributed the vitality and organization of the Guild almost entirely to her. The tribute is justified. During her Secretaryship the Guild grew in numbers from around 1,500 to 52,000, into 'the greatest working women's organization of modern times'. Its carefully orchestrated campaigns included the demands for a minimum wage for Co-operative employees, women's suffrage, the need for better housing, maternity and divorce law reform. The Guild's stand over the last issue cost them, for four years, their four hundred pound subsidy from the Co-op Union, the movement's governing body. Miss Davies herself was always adamant that the Guild must be self-governing and independent – as she put it 'The Guild is looked upon as the left wing of the movement', even as she was to the left both of the movement and of much of organized labour.

A more tangible image of Margaret Llewelyn Davies and a clear indication of her influence on the Guild's style both of organization and campaign comes from her relationships with individual Guild members, the working women from whom she was apparently socially and economically so far distanced. The investigative style of the sanitary inspector never left her, the desire for first-hand information either from her own impressions or preferably from the mouths or pens of those who daily experienced the conditions which needed change. In Sheffield in 1902, trying to spread the Co-operative idea into the poorest areas which had not been touched by the doctrine of organized mutual aid, she went tirelessly round the worst of the slums, noting wages, housing conditions, numbers of children, the feelings of women about their lives. Constantly she emphasized the need to listen to what women said, and to get them to say it for themselves.

There was a warmth and affection about her which never suggested condescension to those less privileged, but rather encouragement and a new hope. The letters which she received from branches all over the country when her retirement was announced in 1921 are not the stale valedictories of an organization to its remote leader. The President of the Plumstead branch, a friend of Miss Davies for twenty years, was 'too full up to speak' when she heard the news; the women of the Rhondda were 'nearly heartbroken'; Sparkhill wrote simply 'The fact is, we all love you, and don't want to lose you.' Similarly, to the young girls of Coronation Street, Sunderland, one of the worst slums in the town where Miss Davies lived for some months in 1902 helping to start a Co-op store and meeting hall, she was a friend, and often a confidante. Jenny Davie, aged seventeen, a tobacco worker, wrote that if she were asked to do 'an exercise about an Ideal Friend, mine will be about you' followed by twenty-nine kisses and the PS 'Write and tell me if you think my writing is getting worse.' Emma Mogg wrote; 'I thank you for your snowdrops and I like your flowers very well, and I will put them in a book for memory of you' followed by twelve kisses.

It was from her time in Sunderland that Miss Davies made earliest reference to her concern with the problems of maternity. Whilst setting up the shop, she one day 'asked a dwarfed girl why she was so small, and she replied "I've been kep' down wi' minding babies! My mother's had thirteen, and I've minded eight.'" In *Maternity* similarly direct stories give a unique source of information and enlightenment. The experience of childbirth for many poor women and their families is summed up in the bald statements at the end of each letter: 'wages 14s, three children, two stillbirths, two miscarriages'; 'wages 18s–22s, eight children, two stillbirths'; 'wages 20s–22s 6d, five children, five stillbirths'.

Although by 1915 obstetric care had advanced to a reasonable standard in some of the better hospitals – the first birth under anaesthesia was in 1847, and antiseptics had reduced a cause of much maternal mortality, puerperal fever – there were few hospital beds for maternity cases in England, and a high level of care was not commonly the experience of the women who wrote the letters. There are frequent references to incompetent or lackadaisical doctors or midwives, the latter having only been formally registered in England from 1902. The birth would take place at home, attended by a doctor, if they could afford one – average cost for a confinement being about £1 1s. Sometimes a midwife at 10s–12s would attend as well, or would do the job single-handedly.

Many could only with difficulty afford these expenses – and wage levels as quoted do not reflect the frequent casuality of a husband's employment. 'I had to do without common necessaries to provide doctor's fees, which so undermined my health that when my baby was born I nearly lost my life ...' '... the doctor's bills grew like mushrooms ...' 'I should say I had a midwife this time, as I could not afford the doctor's fee ...' '... I had hardly enough of anything, let alone a doctor's fee ...'

Skilled medical attention was particularly vital in the case of many of these women because of an almost universal lack of prenatal care. Sometimes this was due to ignorance. Overwhelmingly, poverty was the cause – the experiences described in *Maternity* precede the institution of maternity benefit. Almost every letter reiterates the lack of food, overwork before confinement, and excessively quick return to household chores after birth, as the prime causes of stillbirth and miscarriage, and often lifelong disablement for the mother. One woman whose husband earned 28s a week who had seven children, three stillbirths, four miscarriages, wrote; 'I looked after my husband and children well, but I often went short of food myself, though my husband did not know it. He used to think that my appetite was bad and that I could not eat.' Another, married to a builder's labourer with five children all under eleven years old, worked at a laundry. Ten weeks before her confinement her husband was out of work, so she continued at the laundry until two weeks before the birth; 'None of the previous children are very strong, but what about the last one, with the mother practically starved before birth?'

Enlightened medical opinion agreed that exhaustion

and overwork in the mother contributed highly to the incidence of infant mortality. When the child lived, lack of money to pay for help after the birth often led to serious disability in the mother; 'I used to do my own ironing and knead my bread in bed unknown to the doctor ...' '... I feel sure that if I had had maternity benefit then to help me, I should not be suffering now inwardly ...' '... And now I am suffering myself all from not being able to take care of myself during pregnancy.'

The overall impression from the letters is one of resigned, exhausted endurance. Some confessed to despair; 'My interest in life seemed lost. I was nervous and hysterical; when I walked along the streets I felt that the houses were falling on me, so I took to staying at home, which of course added to the trouble ... Can we any longer wonder why so many married working women are in the lunatic asylums today?'

Yet there are many references, sometimes oblique, which show that many women took a decision not to endure. Mention of birth control is relatively infrequent. The advocation of abstinence, and exhortations to husbands to practise greater self-control, are more usually cited. Above all, a surprising number of the women candidly mention the use of abortifacients, never so named, always called 'drugs'. 'I confess without shame that when well-meaning friends said "you cannot afford another baby, take this drug", I took their strong concoctions to purge me of the little life that might be mine. They failed, as such things generally do.' '... There are three who lost their lives and another who has already had seven. These all took some kind of drug, and of course, it did the work they wanted it to do.'

Most abortifacient drugs available to poor women would only produce abortion as concomitant to the death or serious illness of the women. The kind of remedies available legally over the chemist's counter, Epsom salts, aloes, castor oil, pennyroyal, all kinds of aperients, even various 'female irregularity pills' rarely produced an effect other than nausea.

Infinitely more dangerous, according to various communications to the *British Medical Journal* around 1905–06, were remedies based on a lead substance, diachylon, which affected those who took them with the symptoms of severe lead poisoning, often leading to insanity or death. These pills, often home-made, sometimes distributed by someone with the rudiments of medical knowledge, seem to have been known by different names in different places. In Nottingham, where a successful prosecution was made, Mrs Seagrave's pills were widely used – in Sheffield, Nurse O's pills were made of similar ingredients. Since diachylon could be legally bought over the counter, many women dosed themselves; one woman in Dudley, whose doctor was called after she collapsed, and who subsequently aborted, eventually said she had her 'prescription' from a friend in Manchester: 'Hickey-pickey, bitter apple, bitter aloes, white diachylon – one pennyworth of each.'

As a Sheffield pathologist wrote; 'The news is handed from woman to woman by word of mouth, like any of the other household remedies or "cures" which every woman knows.' The case histories of this desperate underground are tragic, but merely reflect the lengths to which women might go given the conditions of life as described in *Maternity*. One woman wrote; 'Can we wonder that so many women take drugs hoping to get rid of the expected child when they know so little of their own bodies, and have to work so hard to keep, or help to keep, the children they have already got?'

A work, to be propagandist, need not be all gloom. The hope for better things for the next generation, a faith and confidence in the Guild – 'It was the Women's Co-operative Guild that saved me from despair' – pervades many of the letters.

Reforms achieved did not satisfy the Guild. In 1927–28 they were still preparing detailed notes for local speakers on ante-natal care, since the fall in maternal mortality had not reached expectation. Miss Davies was never satisfied: in the 1920s she became increasingly interested in the controversial topic of birth control as the means towards 'a new outlook on marriage, sex and parental relationships'. Yet the Guild's scheme for maternity care sketched in the outlines of the present system of social welfare for mothers, so their faith was never misplaced. One of the contributors to the book wrote; 'If there is anything else you would like to know and I could tell you, I should be glad for the benefit of my sisters.'

Further biographical detail on Miss Margaret Llewelyn Davies is to be found in the *Dictionary of Labour Biography*: Vol. 1 (1972) ed. J. M. Bellamy and J. Saville.

Gloden Dallas was a social historian, the co-author of *The Unknown Army: Mutinies in the British Army in World War I* (Verso, 1985), with Douglas Gill. A mother of three, she studied and supported the women's movement throughout her life.

LIFE AS WE HAVE KNOWN IT
Voices of Working Class Women

Edited by Margaret Llewelyn Davies

'I was born in Bethnal Green . . . a tiny scrap of humanity.
I was my mother's seventh, and seven more were born
after me . . . When I was ten years old I began to earn
my own living.'

Told in the distinctive and memorable voices of working
class women, *Life as We Have Known It* is a remarkable
first-hand account of working lives at the turn of the last
century. First published in association with the Women's
Co-operative Guild in 1931, *Life as We Have Known It* is a
unique evocation of a lost age, and a humbling testament to
what Virginia Woolf called 'that inborn energy which no
amount of childbirth and washing up can quench'. Here is
domestic service; toiling in factories and in the fields, and of
husbands – often old and ill before their time, some
drinkers or gamblers.

Despite telling of the hardship of a poverty-stricken
marriage, the horrors of childbirth and of lives spent in
search of jobs, these are spirited and inspiring voices.